City & Guilds

Level 1 Certificate for IT Users

Spreadsheets

Level

1

Susan Ward

City&
Guilds

Heinemann Educational Publishers
Halley Court, Jordan Hill, Oxford, OX2 8EJ
Part of Harcourt Education

Heinemann is the registered trademark of Harcourt Education Ltd

© Susan Ward, 2002

First published in 2002
2005   2004   2003
10 9 8 7 6 5 4 3 2

A catalogue record for this book is available from the British Library on request.

ISBN 0 435 46262 8

Typeset by Techset Ltd, Gateshead
Printed and bound in UK by Thomson Litho Ltd.

Tel: 01865 888058 www.heinemann.co.uk

Contents

Introduction

City & Guilds e-Quals is an exciting new range of IT qualifications developed with leading industry experts. These comprehensive, progressive awards cover everything from getting to grips with basic IT to gaining the latest professional skills.

The range consists of both user and practitioner qualifications. User qualifications (Levels 1–3) are ideal for those who use IT as part of their job or in life generally, while practitioner qualifications (Levels 2–3) have been developed for those who need to boost their professional skills in, for example, networking or software development.

e-Quals boasts online testing and a dedicated website with news and support materials and web-based training. The qualifications reflect industry standards and meet the requirements of the National Qualifications Framework.

With e-Quals you will not only develop your expertise, you will gain a qualification that is recognised by employers all over the world.

The spreadsheet unit is organised into five outcomes. You will learn to:

- use a spreadsheet software package in its operating environment
- design a simple spreadsheet
- create simple spreadsheets and enter data
- edit spreadsheets and modify cells and ranges of cells
- save, retrieve and print the contents of spreadsheet files.

You do not need any previous experience of using spreadsheets. You will learn the practical skills and the knowledge to go with them. This book covers all the learning points within the outcomes. The 'Outcomes matching guide', at the end of the book, gives the outcomes in full and relates each learning point to the section of the book where it is covered.

Your tutor will give you a copy of the outcomes, so that you can sign and date each learning point as you master the skills and knowledge.

There are five main sections in this book. Each section contains information and practical tasks. There is a detailed method to guide you when you first learn to carry out each task. There are also some hints and reminders at intervals. At the end of a section you will have a chance to practise your skills, check your knowledge, or both. Consolidation exercises provide further practice. Finally you will be able to complete practice assignments which cover a range of skills and are designed to be similar in style to the City & Guilds assignment for the unit.

There are some solutions to the 'Practise your skills' and 'Check your knowledge' questions at the end of the book. There is also a quick reference guide giving alternative methods of carrying out common tasks.

In order to give detailed methods for each task it is necessary to refer to a specific spreadsheet application, though the City & Guilds unit is not specific and can be completed using any spreadsheet application. This book refers to Microsoft Excel 2000, which is the spreadsheet application in the Microsoft Office 2000 suite.

Section 1 | Spreadsheets, software and hardware

Information: What is a spreadsheet?

A **spreadsheet** is a grid of rows and columns. It is used for entering text and numbers and for carrying out calculations. The original spreadsheets were on paper. Computerised spreadsheets have a great advantage because you can change the numbers and the computer will calculate the new results. Business people use spreadsheets for recording and calculating sales figures, expenses and wages, for making invoices, budgets, business plans and much more. Scientists and engineers use spreadsheets for calculations and analysis. People at home use spreadsheets for working out personal finance and taxes.

Hardware and software requirements for spreadsheets

Software

Software is the name for computer programs. Microsoft Excel is a software **application** for producing and using spreadsheets. It is also known as a spreadsheet package. It is part of the Microsoft Office suite of software. There are other spreadsheet applications, such as Lotus 1-2-3, which are used in a similar way.

A single Excel sheet is called a **worksheet**. Several worksheets can be grouped together in a **workbook** and saved as a file. You may come across the terms 'worksheet' and 'workbook' as you use Excel. In this book the more general term 'spreadsheet' is used, except where there is a need to distinguish between worksheets and workbooks.

Hardware

Computer hardware includes all the items you can see and touch. This section introduces the computer hardware that you need in order to use a spreadsheet application. The City & Guilds e-Quals core unit, *IT Principles*, gives a more detailed description of computer hardware.

In order to use a spreadsheet program you will need:

- the main computer unit
- a monitor
- a keyboard
- a mouse or other pointing device
- a printer.

The keyboard and the mouse are called **input devices** because they are used to put data into the computer system. The monitor and the printer are called **output devices** because they are used to get data out of the computer system.

If you are using a laptop computer then the main unit, the screen, the keyboard and the pointing device will be combined in one unit.

The main unit

The main computer unit contains the processor, the memory and a hard disk drive. Most main units also have a floppy disk drive and at least one CD or DVD drive. Disk drives are **storage devices** because they store data on disks or read stored data from disks.

The monitor

The monitor or visual display unit (VDU) displays your work on a screen. Screen size is measured diagonally, corner to corner. Older monitors may have 15-inch screens. More modern monitors can have 17, 19 or 21-inch screens. The resolution of a screen measures the amount of detail the screen can show. For any given size of screen, the more dots of light (pixels) on a screen, the more detail you can see. The size and resolution of the screen are not as critical for spreadsheet work as they are for graphics, but the display should be clear and not flicker.

The keyboard

The keyboard is for typing in data and commands. A standard keyboard has at least 102 keys, usually more. The keyboard illustrations in this book are of a standard keyboard. Laptop computers have compact keyboards with fewer keys.

The pointing device

A pointing device lets you move a pointer on the screen and lets you click buttons to give commands. The mouse is a common pointing device, but there are others, such as trackerballs. Laptop computers often have a touchpad or a small joystick as their pointing device. This book will refer to the mouse, but you can use any other pointing device instead. The left button is used more often than the right. The instruction 'click' or 'left click' means that you should press and release the left mouse button. 'Double click' means press and release the left mouse button quickly twice while holding the mouse still. 'Right click' means press and release the right mouse button. Some designs of mouse have a scroll wheel or additional buttons. You will just be using the left button and occasionally the right button.

The printer

The printer produces hard copy. Hard copy is the name given to computer output on paper. There are black and white printers and colour printers. Many people have inkjet printers at home, while laser printers are common in offices, colleges and schools. Any kind of printer should be suitable for printing out a spreadsheet.

If you are in a college, a school or a training centre then you may be using a networked computer, linked to other computers. You will probably be sharing a printer, which may be some distance away from your computer.

Information: Health and safety

The City & Guilds e-Quals core unit, *IT Principles*, has a whole section on the important topic of using computers safely and without harming yourself or other people. The issues include:

- electrical safety
- the design and layout of the work area, furniture and equipment
- good working habits.

You should develop the habits of

- sitting with a good posture
- using a correct keyboarding technique
- taking regular breaks away from the computer.

Using spreadsheet software: Excel

Excel is the spreadsheet software you will be using.

Task 1.1 — Start Windows

Method

This depends on the computer system you are using.

If you are using a standalone computer you can probably just switch on and wait. Windows should start up and the desktop should appear.

If you are using a networked computer then you will probably need to log on by typing in an identification and a password. Your tutor will tell you what to do.

This book does not cover the use of the Windows operating system beyond the basics you need in order to use Excel. The core unit, *IT Principles*, includes the use of Windows.

Method

I　Left click with your mouse on the Start button in the lower left corner of your screen. A menu appears as shown in Figure 1.1.

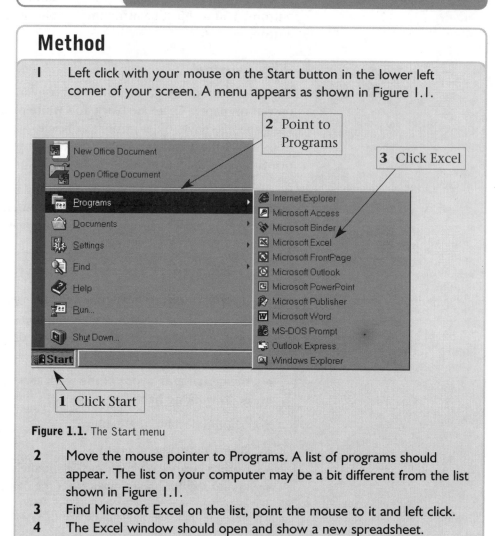

2 Point to Programs

3 Click Excel

1 Click Start

Figure 1.1. The Start menu

2　Move the mouse pointer to Programs. A list of programs should appear. The list on your computer may be a bit different from the list shown in Figure 1.1.

3　Find Microsoft Excel on the list, point the mouse to it and left click.

4　The Excel window should open and show a new spreadsheet.

Information: A quick way of loading Excel

There may be an icon on your Windows desktop that gives a short cut to Excel. If so, you can double click on the icon to start Excel. This is quicker than using the Start button.

Task 1.3　Look at the Excel window

Figure 1.2 shows the parts of the Excel window. Some features will be familiar if you have used other applications such as Microsoft Word. Many applications are deliberately designed to be as similar as possible.

1　The title bar shows the name of the application and the name of the current spreadsheet file. Book 1 is a name given by Excel to a new spreadsheet file. At the right-hand end of the title bar are the window control buttons. These buttons allow you to maximise the window to fill the screen, minimise it down to a button at the bottom of the screen, restore it to its former size, or close the window.

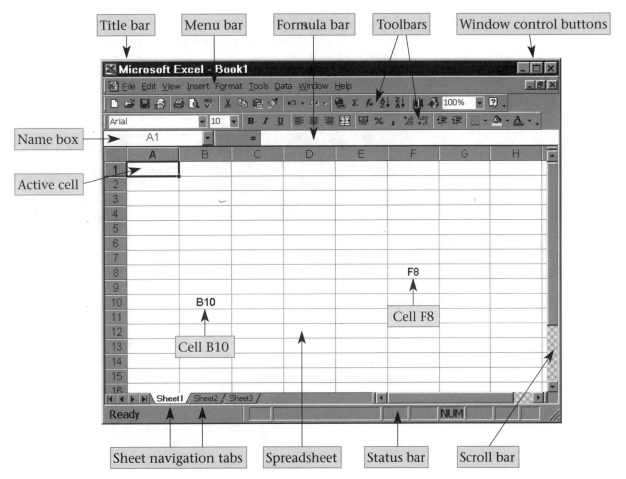

Figure 1.2 The Excel window

2 The menu bar gives a list of drop down menus: File, Edit, and so on. Left click on one of the menu names to see a list of commands. At first you may only see the commands that have been used most recently, as in Figure 1.3. After a few seconds the full list will show. To see the full list more quickly, click on the double arrow. To close a menu without giving a command, either click on the menu name again or click anywhere on the spreadsheet grid.

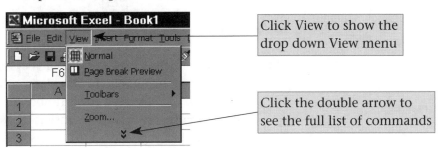

Figure 1.3 A menu showing recently used commands

Practise clicking on menu names to show and hide the drop down menus of commands.

3 Toolbars hold rows of buttons. These give short cuts to some of the more frequently used commands. You may find that the Standard toolbar and the Formatting toolbar are displayed in the same row, as shown in Figure 1.4. There is not enough room to display all the buttons, so only the most recently used buttons are shown. You can see the other buttons by

left clicking on the double arrow to the right of a toolbar. Older versions of Excel showed the toolbars on separate rows so that all the buttons were displayed.

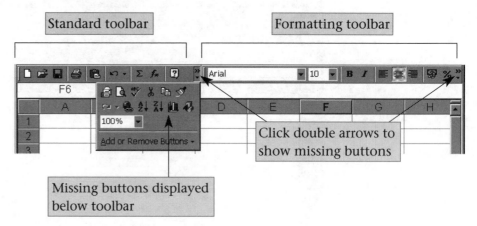

Figure 1.4 Displaying missing toolbar buttons

4 Scroll bars are used to move sideways or up and down on a worksheet. Only a small part of a worksheet is shown on the screen at one time. See Figure 1.5.

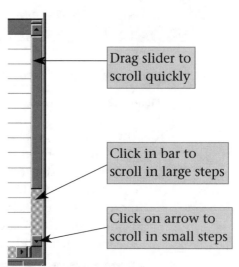

Figure 1.5 A scroll bar

5 The spreadsheet itself is called a **worksheet** in Excel. It consists of a grid of rectangles called **cells**. Each column of cells is headed by a letter. Each row of cells has a row number on the left. Each cell is identified by its **cell reference** which consists of its column letter followed by its row number, e.g. A1, G5, B7. Cells F8 and B10 are shown with their references in Figure 1.2.

6 The **active cell** is the cell that is selected now. It has a dark border. When you key in data, it goes into the active cell. You can select any cell and make it into the active cell. In a new spreadsheet, cell A1 starts as the active cell.

7 Excel saves its spreadsheet files as **workbooks**. A workbook can have several worksheets. Figure 1.2 shows a workbook with three worksheets. The sheet navigation tabs let you switch from one worksheet to another. We shall only be using one worksheet in each workbook.

Task 1.4   Customise the Excel window

The Excel window should fill the whole screen so that you have as much working space as possible. If the window does not fill the screen then maximise it.

Method

I   Click the maximise button. This is the middle of the three buttons in the top right corner of the window. See Figure 1.6.

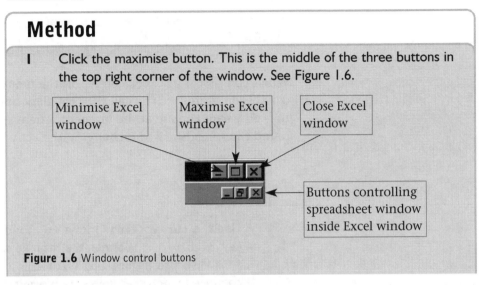

Figure 1.6 Window control buttons

Many people find it easier to work with complete menus and toolbars displayed on the screen. If your version of Excel is displaying only the most recently used menu options and toolbar buttons then change it to show full menus and toolbars.

Method

1   Click on the Tools menu name and select Customise from the drop down list.
2   In the Customise dialogue box (Figure 1.7) click the Options tab to bring it to the front.
3   Click in the check boxes labelled 'Standard and Formatting toolbars share one row' and 'Menus show recently used commands first' to remove the ticks.
4   Click Close.

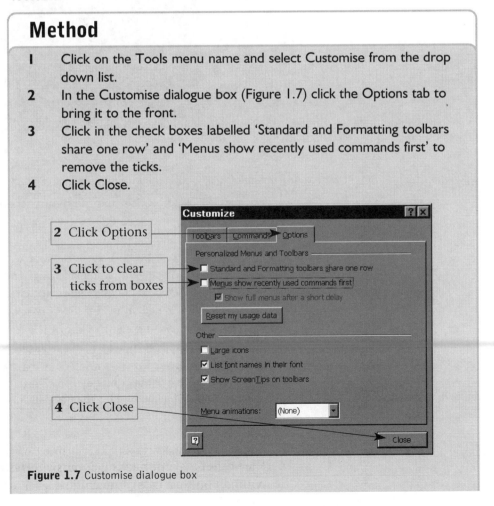

Figure 1.7 Customise dialogue box

You should now see two full toolbars at the top of the screen. When you click a menu name to show the drop down menu, all the commands should be visible straight away.

Task 1.5 — Moving about the spreadsheet

When you first start Excel, cell A1 on the new spreadsheet should have a dark border round it. The cell with the dark border is the active cell, that is, the cell where you are at the moment. There are several ways of moving round the spreadsheet and changing the active cell.

Methods

1   **Use the cursor (arrow) keys to move.** These are the group of four keys with arrows between the main keys and the numeric keypad on a full keyboard (Figure 1.8). On a laptop computer, these keys will be combined with other keys. Try moving to the right, down, then left and up, back to cell A1.

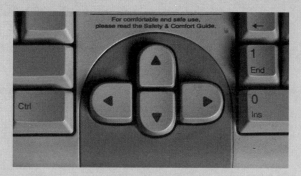

Figure 1.8 Cursor keys

2   **Use the mouse to move.** Point the mouse to the centre of any cell and left click. Notice that the mouse pointer appears as a white cross when it is pointing to the centre of a cell. Move back to cell A1 by clicking.

3   **Use the scroll bars.** The worksheet is much bigger than the area shown on the screen. Scroll sideways and down, find cell R40 and click in it. Scrolling by itself does not change the active cell. You have to click in the cell you want. Scroll back and click in cell A1.

4   **Use the name box** at the left of the formula bar, just below the toolbars (see Figure 1.2). The name box shows the reference of your active cell, so it should show A1 at the moment. Click with the mouse in the name box, key in **N5** and press the Enter key. You should move to cell N5. Use the name box to move back to cell A1.

There are other ways of moving about, but these should be sufficient. Use the method you find most convenient.

Task 1.6   How big is an Excel worksheet?

Method

1. Scroll sideways and find column Z. Continue sideways and you will see that the columns go on with AA, AB and so on. After AZ comes BA. Keep going . . . When you are tired of scrolling, take a short cut to the end. Hold down the control (Ctrl) key on the keyboard while you press the right cursor key. You should find yourself in column IV, the last column. There are 256 columns.

2. Scroll downwards. When you are tired of scrolling, take a short cut to the bottom row. Hold down the control key while you press the down cursor key. The current version of Excel has 65536 rows.

3. That makes 16,777,216 cells. You would never need to use them all. You do not need to worry about running out of space for your spreadsheet.

4. Go back to cell A1. Either hold down the control key while you press the up and left cursor keys or use the name box.

Task 1.7   Move between worksheets in a workbook

Method

1. You have been using Sheet 1. Click on the sheet navigation tab for Sheet 2, near the bottom of the screen, and Sheet 2 will be the active sheet. The tab of the active sheet is white, the other tabs are grey. Click back to Sheet 1.

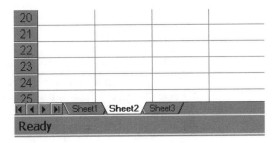

Figure 1.9 Sheet navigation tabs

Task 1.8 — Open more workbooks and move between them

Method

1 Click on the New button on the Standard toolbar

2 Look at the name bar at the top of the window to check that you have a new spreadsheet workbook. Excel should have given it the name Book 2.

3 Click on the Window menu to show the drop down list. Both spreadsheet workbooks should be listed (Figure 1.10). Click on Book 1 to make it active and display it on the screen.

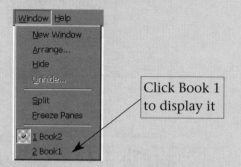

Figure 1.10 The Window menu

4 If both Book 1 and Book 2 are shown on the taskbar at the bottom of the screen, then you can click on the name of the workbook that you want to display. Practise swapping between Book 1 and Book 2. Check the title bar to see which one is displayed.

Task 1.9 — Close down a spreadsheet workbook

Method

1 Click on the File menu and select Close from the drop down list.
2 You may see a message asking if you want to save changes. Click on No.
3 One workbook should close, but the other should still be open.

Task 1.10 — Close down Excel

When you close down Excel, any open workbooks will be closed down too.

Method

1 Click on the File menu and select Exit from the drop down list.
2 You may see a message asking if you want to save changes. Click on No.

If you are working on a networked computer, your tutor will tell you how to **log off**. Logging off finishes your session on the computer system.

If you are working on a standalone computer, you may need to close it down.

Method

1	Click the Start button in the lower left corner of the screen.
2	Select Shut Down from the menu.
3	The Shut Down Windows dialogue box appears. Confirm that Yes, you do want to shut down the computer.
4	After a short time a message may appear on the screen saying that it is safe to switch off the computer. Some systems automatically shut down without showing this message.

Information: Logging off

If you are using a networked computer system, it is important that you log off correctly before you leave the computer. Usually you do this by clicking a button labelled Log off. There will probably be a message asking you to confirm that you really do want to log off. You say yes. The computer system then finishes your session and gets ready for the next person to log on.

You probably have your own file storage area where you will keep your work. If you forget to log off, then the next person who uses the computer will be able to look at all your work, and could damage or delete it. Log off every time. You can then be fairly confident that your work is kept safe and private.

→ Check your knowledge

1 What is the main advantage of a computerised spreadsheet over a spreadsheet on paper?

2 Name two spreadsheet applications.

3 What are the two items of computer hardware that you need for entering data and giving commands?

4 What size of monitor are you using?

5 What kind of printer are you using?

6 What is hard copy?

7 Are you using a standalone computer or a networked computer?

8 What does Excel call a group of worksheets that can be saved together in a file?

9 Which two toolbars would you expect to see near the top of the Excel window?

10 What simple precaution can you take to avoid eyestrain?

Creating a new spreadsheet

You will learn to

- Create a new spreadsheet
- Enter text into spreadsheet cells
- Enter numbers into spreadsheet cells
- Enter simple formulas into spreadsheet cells
- Use the SUM function
- Save a spreadsheet
- Print a spreadsheet showing results
- Print a spreadsheet showing formulas
- Save a copy of a spreadsheet on a floppy disk
- Close a spreadsheet

In Section 1 you explored Microsoft Excel and looked at some empty workbooks and worksheets. In this section you will create several small spreadsheets, save them and print them. You will use the most common types of calculation. The **Fruit spreadsheet** uses adding to find the cost of buying fruit, and subtracting to work out the change. The **Budget spreadsheet** uses a special method for adding several numbers and it also uses dividing. The **Invoice spreadsheet** uses adding again and introduces multiplying.

Fruit spreadsheet

You will create a spreadsheet to find the total cost of buying some apples and pears. The spreadsheet also works out the change to be given when the buyer hands over a £10 note.

Task 2.1   Create a new spreadsheet

Method

| I | Load Excel. A new empty spreadsheet should automatically appear. |

Your new empty spreadsheet should look just like the spreadsheet you created and looked at in Section 1. The title bar at the top should display 'Microsoft – Excel Book1'. You may need to customise the Excel window again as you did in Task 1.4. Some computer systems will save your customised settings from one session to the next. Other systems will not, so that you have to customise every time.

Task 2.2 — Enter text into spreadsheet cells

Hint:

There are two Enter keys on a standard keyboard. One is on the numeric keypad at the right of the keyboard and is usually labelled Enter. The other Enter key is on the main area of the keyboard, and

 is a large key labelled with a bent arrow. It is also known as the Return key.

Figure 2.2 Enter key

Both keys have the same effect. If you are typing text or numbers using the main area of the keyboard then use the Enter key on the main area of the keyboard because it is easier to reach.

Method

1. Check that cell A1 is the active cell. It should have a dark border round it.
2. Key in FRUIT.
   Cell A1 should show the word FRUIT followed by a flashing cursor. The formula bar should show the word FRUIT too. A green tick and a red cross also show to the left of the formula bar (see Figure 2.1). Your text is not yet properly entered into the cell because Excel does not know that you have finished keying in the entry.

A1	▼	✗ ✓ =	FRUIT	◄—— Formula bar

	A	B	C	D
1	FRUIT			
2				

Figure 2.1 Entering text

3. Press the Enter key on the keyboard.
   Several things happen. Your entry is fixed in cell A1 and the flashing cursor disappears. The green tick and the red cross disappear from the formula bar. Probably the active cell will move down one space to A2 (though this depends on how your version of Excel is set up). The contents of A1 no longer show in the formula bar because A1 is no longer the active cell.

Hint:

Instead of pressing Enter to fix data in a cell, you can click with the mouse on the green tick in the formula bar. If you use the tick then the active cell stays where it is instead of moving down.

Task 2.3 — Enter more text

Method

1. In cell A2, key in the word **Apples** and then press Enter.
2. In cell A3, key in the word **Pears** and then press Enter.

Task 2.4 — Enter numbers into spreadsheet cells

Method

1. Go to cell B2 and key in **3.75** then press Enter.
2. In cell B3 key in **5.22** then press Enter or click the green tick.

Task 2.5 — Enter more text and numbers

Method

1   Enter further text and numbers until your spreadsheet looks like Figure 2.3.

	A	B
1	FRUIT	
2	Apples	3.75
3	Pears	5.22
4	Total	
5	Tendered	10
6	Change	
7		

Figure 2.3 The Fruit spreadsheet

2   Go to cell A9 and key in your name. Press Enter.

Hint:

Put your name on every spreadsheet you create. This will be useful when you print the spreadsheet. If you share a printer then you will need to know which printouts are yours.

Information: Text and numbers

You can make three different kinds of entries into a spreadsheet: text, numbers and formulas. So far you have met text and numbers.

Text, or labels, can contain any characters: letters, numbers and punctuation marks.

A **number**, or value, can be a whole number, a number with decimal places, a sum of money, a date, a time or a percentage. Another name for a whole number is **integer**.

Numbers can be used in calculations, but text cannot.

A number cannot contain a space.

Generally a number cannot contain letters or punctuation, but there are a few special cases. These include a single decimal point, a minus sign, a £ sign, a % sign, slash marks in a date and a colon in a time of day.

These can be numbers: 3   5.83   −4.2   £21   5/12/02   9:30   4%
These are not numbers: 6min   2kg   3252a   34/23/02

By default, text is aligned to the left in a cell, but a number is aligned to the right.

Hint:

You are likely to meet the word **default** quite often. It means the normal state: the state that exists if you do not make any changes.

Task 2.6 — Enter simple formulas into spreadsheet cells

A **formula** is an instruction showing how a calculation must be carried out. It starts with the sign =

You need a formula that will find the numbers from cells B2 and B3, add them, and put the result in cell B4.

Method

1   Go to cell B4 and key in **=B2+B3** then press Enter.
2   Check the result shown in cell B4. It should be 8.97.
3   Move back to cell B4 and look at the formula bar above the main spreadsheet area. The formula bar shows the formula, but the cell shows the result.

You need a formula in cell B6 that will work out the change from £10.

Remember:

A cell reference is used to identify a particular cell. The cell reference consists of the column letter and the row number. B4 and B5 are cell references.

Method

1   Go to cell B6 and key in **=B5−B4**
2   Check that the result is right. It should be 1.03.

Information: Arithmetic signs

The signs for add and subtract are the same as the ones we use when writing. The signs for multiply and divide are different.

\+   add   −   subtract   *   multiply   /   divide

Task 2.7   Save a spreadsheet

Method

1   Click the Save button on the Standard toolbar
2   The Save As dialogue box appears (Figure 2.4).
3   Give your spreadsheet the file name **Fruit**.
4   Look at the box labelled Save as Type. It should tell you that the file will be saved as an Excel workbook.
5   Look at the box labelled Save in. This shows the folder where your file will be saved. You may be saving into the My Documents folder, or your tutor may tell you to save your files in a different folder.
6   Click Save.

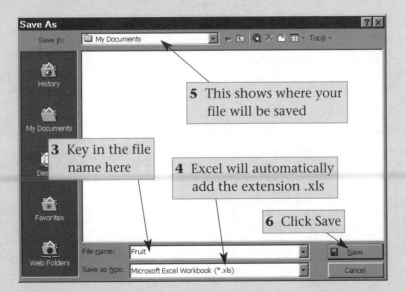

Figure 2.4 Save As dialogue box

Information

Saving to disk

While you are working, your spreadsheet and everything you key into it are held in the computer's **main memory** (RAM). This is a volatile, temporary memory. It loses all its contents when the power supply is turned off.

In order to keep your spreadsheet, you must save it as a file into long-term storage. This will normally be on a **hard disk**. On a standalone computer your files are saved on a hard disk hidden inside the main computer unit. If you are on a networked computer then your files are probably saved on a hard disk on a central computer. It is also possible to save files on a removable **floppy disk**. Your tutor will tell you if you need to use floppy disks.

Folders (Directories)

Files are organised into **folders** on a disk. Figure 2.4 shows the Fruit.xls file being saved into a folder called My Documents. If you are working in a college, school or training centre, then you may be asked to save files into a particular folder. You may come across the word **directory**. This is another name for a folder.

File names

Every file must have a name. The main part of the name is followed by a dot and three characters called the **extension**. The extension tells the computer system what kind of data is stored in the file. Excel saves its spreadsheet files as workbooks with the extension **.xls**.

You can choose the main part of the name. It should remind you what is in the file. Modern computer systems allow long file names that can contain letters, numbers and spaces. Some punctuation marks are allowed but others are not. You may find it simpler to avoid using punctuation marks in file names. Some older systems allowed only 8 characters with no spaces.

When you saved your Fruit spreadsheet, you gave it the name Fruit. Excel automatically added the extension .xls. The full name of your spreadsheet is therefore Fruit.xls.

Task 2.8 — Print a spreadsheet showing results

Method

1 Click the Print Preview button on the toolbar

2 Check the layout of your spreadsheet on the preview screen. Click on the spreadsheet to zoom in for a closer look. Click again to zoom out.

3 Check the Previous and Next buttons near the top of the screen. These should both have pale grey text, showing that there is no previous page and no next page.

4 If you are satisfied, click the Print button on the preview screen. If you decide not to print, then click the Close button to leave Print Preview (see Figure 2.5).

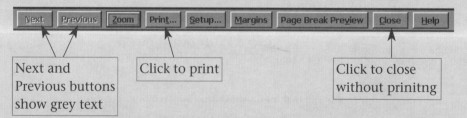

Figure 2.5 Buttons in Print Preview window

5 Do not change any settings in the Print dialogue box. Just click OK.

Task 2.9 — Print a spreadsheet showing formulas

Method

1. Start with your Fruit spreadsheet displayed normally on the screen.
2. Click on the Tools menu and select Options from the drop down list.
3. The View tab may already be in front (Figure 2.6). If not, click on the View tab.
4. Click in the check box labelled Formulas.

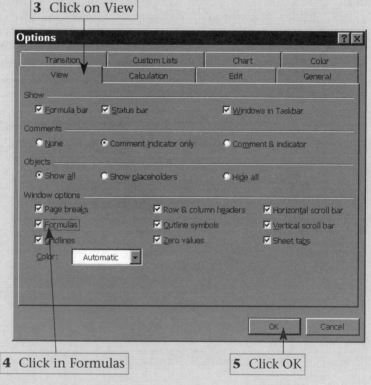

Figure 2.6 Options dialogue box

5. Click OK. You should see formulas in cells B4 and B6.
6. Click the Print Preview button on the toolbar.
7. Click Print to print the spreadsheet showing formulas.

Task 2.10 — Return to the Normal view of the spreadsheet

Method

1. Click on the Tools menu and select Options from the drop down list.
2. The View tab should be in front. Click in the check box labelled Formulas to remove the tick.
3. Click OK.

Information: Cell contents and appearance

The display in a spreadsheet cell (its **appearance**) may not be the same as the data stored in that cell (its **contents**).

Cell B4 of your spreadsheet stores the formula =B2+B3 but it normally displays the result of that formula, not the formula itself.

When you view the formulas, the formulas are displayed in their cells, and they can be printed out.

Some other aspects of the display may change, for example numbers may align to the left instead of the right.

You will normally be asked to print at least two copies of each spreadsheet, one showing results and one showing formulas.

Cells become wider when you view formulas. They become narrower again when you go back to view the results.

Task 2.11　Save a spreadsheet again

Your spreadsheet has already been saved and given a name. You will now save it again, replacing the previous version.

Method

I　Click the Save button on the toolbar.
There is no dialogue window this time to show that the file is being saved. If you watch the status bar at the bottom of the screen you might see a message flash up as you click Save, but it happens very quickly.

Task 2.12　Close a spreadsheet

Method

I　Click on the File menu and select Close from the drop down list.

Information: Another way to close a spreadsheet

You can also close a spreadsheet by clicking the X button in the top right corner of its window. There may be two X buttons. The lower button belongs to the spreadsheet, and this is the one you should click. The upper button belongs to Excel itself and will close down the whole program. If you close Excel by mistake, do not worry. Just load it again.

Budget spreadsheet

You will create a spreadsheet to add up the monthly household bills for a flat. Two people are sharing the flat, so the spreadsheet will divide the cost by two to find out how much each person should pay. Most of what you do will be revision of methods you learned for the Fruit spreadsheet. New topics are:

- Using the SUM function
- Dividing
- Showing gridlines and row/column headings when you print.

Task 2.13   Create a spreadsheet

Method

I   Find and click the New button on the Standard toolbar.

Task 2.14   Save the spreadsheet

Method

I   Click the Save button on the Standard toolbar.
2   The Save As dialogue will appear. Give your spreadsheet the name Budget and click Save.

Hint:

It is a good idea to save a spreadsheet and give it a name before you start entering data. You should then save frequently as you work. If there is a power cut or the computer crashes, you should be able to get back the work you have saved. Anything you have not saved may be lost.

Task 2.15   Enter text and numbers

Method

I   Enter text and numbers as shown in Figure 2.7. Add your own name in cell A13.

	A	B	
1	Budget		
2			
3		April	
4	Rent	425	
5	Council	64	
6	Electricity	25	
7	Gas	20	
8	Phone	32	
9	Total		
10			
11	Share		
12			

Figure 2.7 Budget spreadsheet

Task 2.16 — Use the SUM function to add numbers

You could add up the total by using the formula =B4+B5+B6+B7+B8.

There is a better way using the SUM function.

Method

1. Go to cell B9.
2. Find and click the Autosum button on the toolbar Σ
3. Autosum offers the formula **=SUM(B4:B8)** in cell B9.
4. Check that the right cells are being added, B4 to B8 inclusive.
5. Press Enter to accept the formula.

Information: The SUM function

The SUM function is used in a formula when you want to add up the contents of several cells.

You can key the formula **=SUM(B4:B8)** in yourself instead of using the Autosum button.

Sometimes Autosum will not choose the right cells for you, and you will need to correct the formula or key it in yourself.

The formula starts in the usual way with =.

The function starts with its name, SUM.

In round brackets after the function name are the cells that the function must use.

B4:B8 is the **range** of cells B4 to B8 inclusive. The symbol between B4 and B8 is the colon (:).

The SUM function is for adding. Do not use it if you want to subtract, multiply or divide.

There are other functions, but SUM is the most commonly used function.

Task 2.17 — Enter a simple formula into a spreadsheet cell – division

Hint:

Remember that the symbol for divide is /

The total needs to be divided by 2 to find how much each person must pay.

Method

1. Go to cell B11.
2. Key in the formula **=B9/2**
3. Press Enter

Task 2.18 Save a spreadsheet

The spreadsheet has been saved and named, but save it again now.

Method

I   Click the Save button on the toolbar.

Task 2.19 Print a spreadsheet showing results

Method

1   Click the Print Preview button on the toolbar.
2   Check the display in the Preview window.
3   Click the Print button.
4   Click OK in the Print dialogue box.

Task 2.20 Print a spreadsheet showing formulas

Method

1   Click on the Tools menu and select Options from the drop down list.
2   Click on the View tab if it is not already in front.
3   Click in the check box labelled Formulas.
4   Click OK.
5   Preview, check and print the spreadsheet.

Information: Showing formulas with a hotkey

There is a quick method of swapping between showing results and showing formulas in cells, using a hotkey or keyboard shortcut.

Find the key on the left of the keyboard, next to the 1 key in the numbers row. It shows ` and 2 other symbols. See Figure 2.8.

Hold down the Crtl key as you press this ` key.

The view swaps between results and formulas. Press again to swap back.

Key for showing and hiding formulas

Figure 2.8 Key for showing formulas

Task 2.21 Print gridlines and row/column headings

By default, the spreadsheet gridlines and the row and column headings do not print out. It can be useful to print them in draft versions of a spreadsheet, and also when you print showing formulas.

Method

1   Click on the File menu and select Page Setup from the drop down list.
2   Click on the Sheet tab in the Page Setup dialogue box (Figure 2.9).
3   Click in the check boxes labelled Gridlines and Row and column headings to place ticks.
4   Click Print Preview.
5   Click the Print button in the preview window.

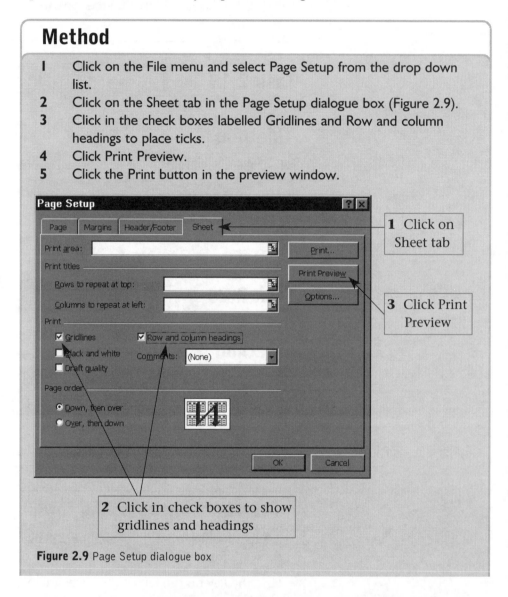

1 Click on Sheet tab

3 Click Print Preview

2 Click in check boxes to show gridlines and headings

Figure 2.9 Page Setup dialogue box

Hint:

You can go from Print Preview straight to the Page Setup dialogue box. Click the Setup button at the top of the Print Preview window. This is useful if you are not satisfied with the Print Preview display and want to make changes.

Task 2.22 Close a spreadsheet without saving

Method

1   Click on the File menu and select Close from the drop down list.
2   You should see a message asking if you want to save changes.
3   Click No. Your spreadsheet will not be saved again. It will stay as it was when you saved it last.

Clothes invoice spreadsheet

You will prepare a spreadsheet to find the cost of several items of clothing. Most of the tasks are revision. New topics are:

- Use a formula to multiply
- Print in landscape orientation.

Task 2.23 | **Create the spreadsheet, save it, and enter data**

Create a new spreadsheet.
Save the spreadsheet with the name Clothes.
Enter data as shown in Figure 2.10.

	A	B	C	D	E
1	Clothes				
2					
3		VAT rate	17.50%		
4					
5	Code	Item	Price	Quantity	Cost
6	M32	T shirt	6.99	3	
7	M26	Jeans	17.99	2	
8				Subtotal	
9				VAT	
10				Total	
11					

Figure 2.10 Clothes spreadsheet

Task 2.24 | **Enter a simple formula into a spreadsheet cell – multiply**

To find the cost of the T-shirts you multiply the price by the quantity.

Method

1 Go to cell E6.
2 Key in the formula **=C6*D6**
3 Press Enter.

Remember:

The symbol for multiply is *

Task 2.25 Complete the spreadsheet

Hint:

There is another way of putting cell references into a formula, using the mouse instead of the keyboard. Instead of keying in =E8+E9 you would do the following:

Key in =
Click in cell E8
Key in +
Click in cell E9
Press Enter.

If you are keying in a formula and you click into a cell, then the reference of that cell goes into the formula. Take care not to click into a cell by mistake before you have pressed Enter to complete the formula.

Method

1   Go to cell E7 and key in the formula =C7*D7 then press Enter.
2   Go to cell E8 and use the Autosum button to put in the formula =SUM(E6:E7). Remember to press Enter.
3   Go to cell E9. Key in the formula =E8*C3 and press Enter. This multiplies the subtotal by the VAT rate to find the amount of VAT to be paid.
4   Go to cell E10. Key in the formula =E8+E9 and press Enter. This adds the subtotal to the VAT to give the total.
5   Save the spreadsheet again.

The spreadsheet should now look like Figure 2.11.

	A	B	C	D	E
1	Clothes				
2					
3		VAT rate	17.50%		
4					
5	Code	Item	Price	Quantity	Cost
6	M32	T shirt	6.99	3	20.97
7	M26	Jeans	17.99	2	35.98
8				Subtotal	56.95
9				VAT	9.96625
10				Total	66.91625
11					

Figure 2.11 Clothes spreadsheet with results

The VAT and Total figures are not displayed well. They show too many decimal places. In Section 3 you will learn how to improve the display.

Task 2.26 Preview and print the spreadsheet

Method

1   Click the Print Preview button.
2   Check the preview.
3   Click Print, then click OK.

Task 2.27 Print formulas using landscape orientation

Sometimes a spreadsheet is too wide to print on one sheet of paper. A spreadsheet that fits on one sheet in the Normal results view may become too wide when you swap to Formula view. One solution is to change the orientation of the paper.

A sheet of paper with its shorter edge at the top is in portrait orientation. Turn the paper so that its longer edge is at the top, and it is in landscape orientation.

Method

1 View the formulas. Either use Ctrl + ' or click on the Tools menu and select Options from the drop down list, then select View, Formulas, OK.
2 Click the Print Preview button.
3 Inspect the preview window. Probably the Next button is active, with black text. Click on it to see that the spreadsheet goes on to a second page.
4 Close the preview window without printing.
5 Click on the File menu and select Page Setup from the drop down list (Figure 2.12).
6 If the Page tab is not already in front then click on it to bring it to the front.
7 Click on the Landscape option button.
8 Click Print Preview.

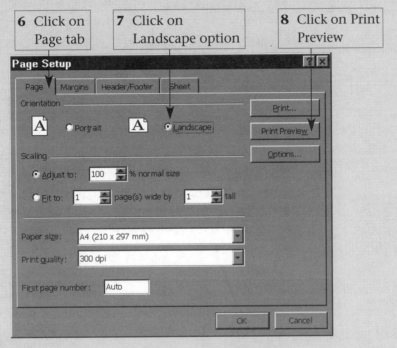

Figure 2.12 Page Setup dialogue box

9 Check the preview window to make sure that the whole spreadsheet now fits on one page.
10 Click Print, then OK.
11 Swap back to the Normal results view.

Information: Saving files on floppy disks

You are probably saving your files on a hard disk. This may be the hard disk in the computer you are using. If you are using a networked computer, it may be a hard disk on a central computer. Hard disks are most convenient for normal working. When you hand in files for marking, and particularly when you do an assignment, your tutor may ask you to save a file to a floppy disk, sometimes called a diskette. Floppy disks are removable, and can be used in another computer. They can also be stored in case your work needs to be checked later.

Floppy disks are also useful for making backup copies of files. A backup is a second copy that you keep in case the original file is lost or damaged. The backup can be restored and used if necessary.

Task 2.28 | Save a copy of the spreadsheet on a floppy disk

To carry out this task you will need a floppy disk that is ready to use and has a label on it.

Method

1 Start with your clothes spreadsheet on the screen.
2 Save the spreadsheet in the usual way using the Save button so that you have the most recent version saved in the usual location on the hard disk.
3 Put the floppy disk in its drive. The label should be uppermost. You should hold the disk label so that the metal slider goes into the drive first. Push the disk in until you hear a click.

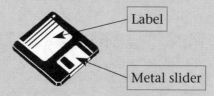

Figure 2.13 Floppy disk

4 Click on the File menu and select Save As from the drop down list. The Save As dialogue box appears.
5 Click on the arrow at the right of the Save in box to show a list of locations where files might be saved. Your list will be different from the one in Figure 2.14. It depends on how your computer system has been set up.

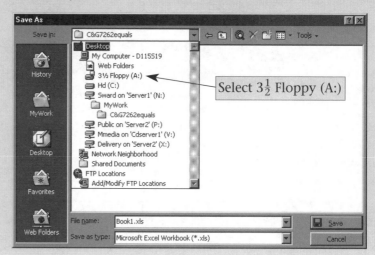

Figure 2.14 Saving to floppy disk

6 Click on 3½ Floppy (A:) from the list to select it.
7 Click Save.
8 Close down Excel.
9 The light on the floppy disk drive may go on again. Wait until it goes out. Press the button on the floppy disk drive to eject the disk. It should pop out so that you can remove it.

Hint:

You should see the floppy disk drive light come on as the file is saved to the floppy disk. Be prepared for the save to take longer than usual. Floppy disks work more slowly than hard disks.

Hint:

Always close down Excel before taking out the floppy disk. The computer does not always finish saving the file completely until you close Excel. If you take the disk out too soon then your file may not be saved properly.

Remember:

Take regular breaks to avoid eyestrain.

→ Practise your skills 1 – Stalls spreadsheet

Here you will set up a spreadsheet to find the profit from stalls at a summer fete.

If you cannot remember the methods, look back at the tasks earlier in this section.

Instructions

1 Load Excel if it is not already open.
2 Create a new spreadsheet.
3 Save the new spreadsheet with the name Stalls.
4 Enter data as shown in Figure 2.15.

	A	B
1	Stalls	
2		
3	Income	
4	Cakes	89.25
5	Plants	62.32
6	Raffle	96.75
7	Tombola	84.35
8	Total	
9		
10	Expenses	
11	Band	57.75
12	Prizes	43.15
13	Tickets	6.35
14	Total	
15		
16	Profit	
17		

Figure 2.15 Stalls spreadsheet

5 In cell B8, enter a formula to find the total income. (**Hint**: use Autosum.)
6 In cell B14, enter a formula to find the total expenses.
7 In cell B16, enter a formula that finds the profit. Profit is Total income – Total expenses.
8 Save the completed spreadsheet.
9 Print the spreadsheet showing the results.
10 Print the spreadsheet showing the formulas, with gridlines and row/column headings. (**Hint**: you need Page Setup for gridlines and headings.)
11 Optional – save a copy of the file on a floppy disk.
12 Close the spreadsheet.

→ Practise your skills 2 – Computer sales spreadsheet

You will set up a spreadsheet to record the sales of different models of computer by two members of the sales staff, and calculate their bonus.

Instructions

1 Load Excel if it is not already open.

2 Create a new spreadsheet.

3 Save the new spreadsheet with the name Computer Sales.

4 Enter data as shown in Figure 2.16.

	A	B	C	D	E	F
1	Sales					
2						
3					Nasir	Sarah
4			Model	System X	25300	21150
5				HomePro	18750	22800
6				Total		
7						
8	Bonus	2%		Bonus		
9						

Figure 2.16 Computer Sales spreadsheet

5 In cell E6 enter a formula to find the total sales made by Nasir.

6 In cell F6 enter a formula to find the total sales made by Sarah.

7 In cell E8 enter a formula to find Nasir's bonus. Multiply his total by the bonus rate in cell B8.

8 In cell F8 enter a formula to find Sarah's bonus.

9 Save the completed spreadsheet.

10 Print the results.

11 Print the formulas on one sheet of paper, showing gridlines and row/column headings. (**Hint**: use landscape orientation.)

12 Optional – save a copy of the file on a floppy disk.

13 Close the spreadsheet. Close Excel.

Remember:

If you are using a floppy disk then close Excel down and wait for the disk drive light to go out before taking the floppy disk out of its drive.

→ Check your knowledge

1 What are the three different kinds of entries you can make into a spreadsheet?

2 Which of the following can be accepted as numbers?
   a   52.43
   b   6 apples
   c   20%
   d   54873a

3 Which character do you key in to start a formula?

4 What formula would you use to multiply the contents of cells C5 and C6?

5 What formula would you use to add the contents of cells D3 to D8 inclusive?

6 What is the symbol that means divide?

7 What is the symbol that means subtract?

8 What extension does Excel add when you save a spreadsheet file?

9 As you work, your spreadsheet is held in the computer's main memory. Why do you need to save your spreadsheet to disk?

10 Paper can be used in two orientations: portrait and . . .

Section 3

Altering an existing spreadsheet

You will learn to

- Open previously prepared spreadsheets
- Use systematic filenames and extensions to save edited spreadsheets
- Use saving processes to prevent loss of work: frequent, automatic
- Edit the contents of individual cells
- Delete cell contents
- Modify cell height and width
- Select cells in spreadsheets using the keyboard and a pointing device
- Align cell contents to left, right and centre
- Modify number formats to general, fixed decimal place, currency and percentage
- Modify text font, size and enhancements (bold, italic)
- Use the undo feature

Fruit spreadsheet

Task 3.1 — Open previously prepared spreadsheet

Method

1 Start Excel.
2 Click the Open button on the toolbar
3 In the Open dialogue box (Figure 3.1), click on the file name Fruit.xls to select it.
4 Click Open. The spreadsheet will open.

Hint:

Instead of clicking once on the filename Fruit.xls then clicking Open, you can double click quickly on the filename to open the file. If you try to double click on the filename but do it too slowly then the system may detect two single clicks instead of a double click. Instead of opening the file, this will select the filename for editing so that you can change the name. To stop this from happening, point the mouse at the little icon just to the left of the filename as you double click.

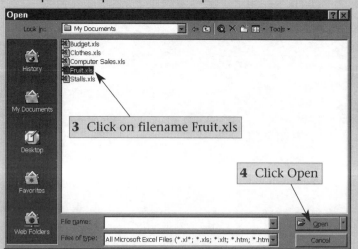

Figure 3.1 Open dialogue box

Task 3.2 — Use systematic filenames to save edited spreadsheets

You are going to make changes to the Fruit.xls spreadsheet. If you make changes and then click the Save button, you will be replacing the old version of the spreadsheet with the new version. Sometimes you may want to do this. At other times you may want to keep the old version as well as the new version.

You will now make a copy of the Fruit.xls spreadsheet and save it with the name Fruit2.xls. You can then make the changes to Fruit2.xls but leave the original version, Fruit.xls, unchanged.

Method

1 Click on the File menu and select Save As from the drop down list.
2 The Save As dialogue box opens. This is the same dialogue box that you see when you save a new spreadsheet for the first time.
3 The Filename box shows Fruit.xls. Key in **Fruit2** instead.
4 Click Save.
5 Look at the name bar at the top of the spreadsheet window. You should see the name Fruit2.xls displayed. This shows that you are now working with the Fruit2 spreadsheet.

Hint:

You could make the changes first and then use Save As to save a new version, but there is a risk that you will do an ordinary save by mistake and replace the old version. It is safer to save the new version with a new name before making any changes.

Information: Spreadsheet versions

When you save different versions of a spreadsheet, you should choose names that show they are versions of the same spreadsheet. One possibility is to use the same name but add a version number: Fruit1, Fruit2, Fruit3 etc. You could use a scheme with dates: SalesFeb2001, SalesMar2001 etc. Whatever scheme you adopt, use filenames that indicate the contents of the spreadsheets.

Task 3.3 — Use saving processes to prevent loss of work: frequent, automatic

You should save frequently as you work by pressing the Save button on the toolbar. Remember that the computer's memory is volatile. It loses all its contents when the power goes off. Any unsaved work will be lost if there is a power cut or a system crash.

You can also set Excel to save your work automatically at regular intervals. The autosave feature is an add-on, not part of the basic Excel application. If it is not available you may need to add it in.

Method

1   Click on the Tools menu and look at all the options. If your menus are set to show the most recently used options first then you will need to wait for a few seconds or click the arrows at the bottom of the menu so that all the options show.
2   If the AutoSave option is on the menu then skip to step 7.
3   If the AutoSave option is not on the menu then select the Add-Ins option.
4   Select the AutoSave Add-in from the list in the Add-Ins dialogue box. Click in the check box to place a tick (Figure 3.2). Click OK.

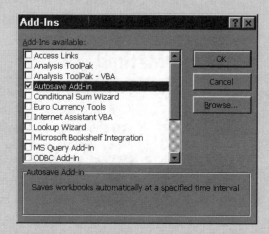

Figure 3.2 Add-Ins dialogue box

5   If the Add-Ins were originally installed with Excel then the AutoSave feature will be made available. If not, you may see a warning message saying 'Microsoft Excel can't run this add-in.' Tell your tutor that Excel does not have AutoSave installed. If you are at home and have the MS Office installation CDs then you could click Yes to the message and follow the instructions on the screen to install the Add-Ins.
6   Assuming that the Add-Ins are installed and that you have selected AutoSave from the Add-Ins dialogue, you are ready to continue. Click on the Tools menu again.
7   Select AutoSave from the drop down list.
8   The AutoSave dialogue box appears (Figure 3.3). Change the automatic save from 10 minutes to 5 minutes. Leave the tick in the Prompt Before Saving box for now.
9   Click OK.

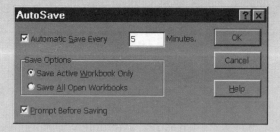

Figure 3.3 AutoSave dialogue box

Carry on with the tasks. Every 5 minutes a message should appear asking if you want to save. Click Save.

If you find the message annoying you can clear the tick in the Prompt Before Saving box. The automatic save will then happen without warning you.

Task 3.4	Edit the contents of individual cells – overtyping

You will change the spreadsheet so that it shows a sale of oranges for 2.95 instead of a sale of apples for 3.75. Before you start, look at the results of the formulas. The total in B4 is 8.97 and the change in B6 is 1.03.

Method

I	Go to cell A2
2	Key in **Oranges**
3	Press Enter
4	Go to cell B2
5	Key in **2.95**
6	Press Enter.

Typing into a cell replaces any existing cell contents. Replacing numbers has another effect too. Look at the total in cell B4. The formula has recalculated the total to show the new value of 8.17. The formula in B6 has recalculated the change to 1.83.

Information: What if?

Formulas recalculate results every time the spreadsheet is changed. This is the feature that makes spreadsheets such a useful tool. It lets the spreadsheet user ask 'What if' and get an answer. What would happen to the business profits if I raised the selling price of an item by 5p? What if sales fell by 2%? What if I gave the staff a pay rise of 3%? The spreadsheet user keys in the new numbers and the answer appears.

Remember:

Save at intervals as you work. Just click the Save button.

Task 3.5	Edit the contents of individual cells – editing in place

Instead of replacing the contents of a cell, you can place a cursor into a cell and change part of the contents.

Method

1. Double click in cell A3. A flashing cursor appears.
2. Move the cursor between the r and the s of Pears. You can use the arrow keys on the keyboard to move the cursor, or you can use the mouse.
3. Use the Backspace delete key to delete the letter r. Backspace delete is the key with the left pointing arrow just above the main Enter key.
4. Key in the letters **che** so that the word is now Peaches.
5. Press Enter.

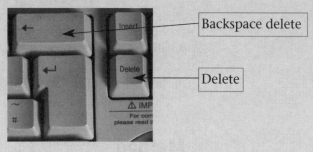

Figure 3.4 Delete and Backspace delete

Task 3.6   Delete cell contents

You will delete the title FRUIT from cell A1.

Method

1. Go to cell A1.
2. Press the Delete key on the keyboard. This time use the key labelled Delete or Del, not the Backspace delete key that you used earlier.

Task 3.7   Modify cell height and width

Up to this point you have been keying in short pieces of text into cells. If you key in longer pieces of text, you may have to make cells wider. You might also want to modify the height and width of cells to improve the display.

First you will see how long text can display across empty cells.

Method

1. Go to cell A1 and key in: **Sales of fruit and change given**.
2. Press Enter.
3. Go to cells A1, B1 and C1 in turn and look at the Formula bar each time. The text is displayed across cells A1, B1 and C1, but it is all stored in A1. Cells B1 and C1 are empty.

Next you will make a cell wider to show text.

Method

1 Go to cell A2 and key in Cape Gooseberries.
2 Press Enter. Only part of the text in A2 is displayed.
3 Point the mouse to the border between the A and B column
   headings. The mouse pointer should change to a vertical line with
   arrows pointing left and right (Figure 3.5).
4 Hold down the left mouse button as you drag the mouse to the right.
   Let go of the button when column A is wide enough to show the
   whole of the entry in cell A2.

	A	B
1		
2	Cape Goo:	2.95
3	Peaches	5.22
4	Total	8.17
5	Tendered	10
6	Change	1.83
7		

Point the mouse here to change column width

Figure 3.5 Change column width

As you drag to make the column wider, a yellow label appears, telling you
the width of the column.

As you make column A wider, column B moves sideways and stays the same
width.

Task 3.8   Select cells in spreadsheets

If you want to make any changes to a spreadsheet cell, you first have to
select it. You select a single cell by moving to it and making it the active
cell. You can also select a range of cells.

Method

1 Point the mouse to the centre of cell B2. The mouse pointer should
   look like a white cross, not an arrow.
2 Hold down the left mouse button and drag the mouse until the
   pointer is in the centre of cell B6. Release the button.
3 The range of cells from B2 to B6 is selected. The background colour
   changes to show this, except for B2 which is the active cell. It is
   selected but it does not change its colour.
4 Deselect the cells by clicking the mouse in any spreadsheet cell.

Hint:

There is an alternative method of changing column width that gives you greater control over the final width. Select any cell in the column you want to change.

Click on the Format menu and select Column from the drop down list, then select Width from the submenu.

A small dialogue box appears. Key in the width you want. Click OK.

Another alternative is to allow Excel to choose the column width to fit the contents. Point the mouse to the border between column headings and double click.

Hint:

A number that is too long for its cell cannot display across adjacent empty cells. Instead the cell will display a row of hash marks #######. This means that the cell must be made wider.

Hint:

You can select cells using the keyboard. Move to the first cell you want to select.

Hold down the Shift key as you move up, down or sideways to the other cells using the cursor arrow keys.

You must start in one corner of the range you want, and move to the opposite corner.

You cannot start in the middle and move out in both directions.

| Task 3.9 | **Align cell contents to left, right and centre** |

Text is left aligned by default, but you can make it right or centre aligned.

Method

1   Select cells A2 to A6.
2   Click the Right Align button on the Formatting toolbar (Figure 3.6).
3   Click in any spreadsheet cell to deselect.

Left align →   ← Right align

Centre

Figure 3.6 Align buttons

Try aligning the text to the centre and back again to the left.

Numbers can be aligned in the same way, but it is best to leave them right aligned.

Information: Number formats

By default, numbers are displayed in general format. They show only what is necessary to display the value. Zeros are not displayed unless they affect the value. If you key in 10.00 or 10.0 or 0010 the cell will display 10.

Fixed Number format will show numbers to a chosen number of decimal places. If you fix the format to show 2 decimal places then 10 will display as 10.00 and 14.2878 will display as 14.29.

Currency or accounting formats will display numbers as currency with a £ sign and with 0 or 2 decimal places. You can also display the euro and other currency signs.

Percentage format shows a number 100 times the stored value, followed by a % sign. If you key in 0.2 in a cell and format it to percentage then it will display 20%.

The display in a cell may not be the same as the cell contents. The cell containing 14.2878 may display 14.29, but the stored value is still 14.2878, and this stored value will be used in any calculations involving the cell. The cell displaying 20% will still store the value 0.2. A cell displaying £52.50 will store the value 52.5.

Modify number formats to general, fixed decimal place, currency and percentage

Method for formatting to a fixed number of decimal places

1   Select cells B2 to B6.
2   Click on the Format menu and select Cells from the drop down list.
3   The Number tab should be in front. If it is not, then click on it (Figure 3.7).
4   Select Number from the Category list.
5   Set the number of decimal places to 2.
6   Click OK.

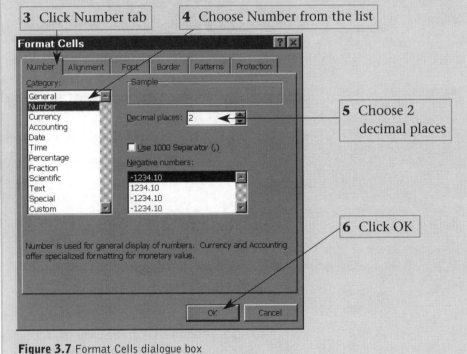

3 Click Number tab   **4** Choose Number from the list

5 Choose 2 decimal places

6 Click OK

Figure 3.7 Format Cells dialogue box

Method for formatting to currency

1   Select cells B2 to B6.
2   Click on the Format menu and select Cells from the drop down list.
3   The Number tab should be in front. If it is not, then click on it.
4   Select Currency from the Category list.
5   Set the number of decimal places to 2.
6   Click OK.

Hint:

There are some shortcut buttons on the Formatting toolbar (Figure 3.8). Use these to format numbers quickly to currency or to increase or decrease the number of decimal places to be displayed.

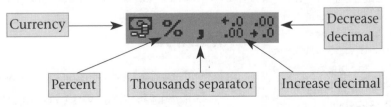

Currency   Decrease decimal

Percent   Thousands separator   Increase decimal

Figure 3.8 Number format buttons

Task 3.11 — Modify text font, size and enhancements (bold, italic)

You can improve the appearance of a spreadsheet and make it clearer by altering the font type and size or by using bold or italic.

Method

1　Select cell A1.
2　On the Formatting toolbar, click the arrow to show the Font Size drop down list (Figure 3.9).
3　Select size 14 from the drop down list.
4　Select cells A2 to A6.
5　Click the Italic button on the Formatting toolbar.
6　Select cells A4 and B4.
7　Click the Bold button on the Formatting toolbar.
8　Select cell A1 again.
9　Click the arrow to show the Font drop down list.
10　Select a font from the list. Different fonts are available on different systems, so experiment until you find a font that looks suitable for the title.

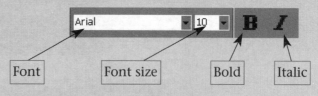

Font　　　Font size　　　Bold　　　Italic

Figure 3.9 Font formatting

Information: Fonts

Arial font is commonly used in spreadsheets because it is clear and easy to read. Other fonts can be used to emphasise titles or to give a different effect. Some fonts look like handwriting or calligraphy. Some are meant to look old-fashioned, some look modern. Some are formal, some are more casual. Explore the range of fonts available to you on your computer system. Use fonts that are easy to read, particularly for numbers. Avoid mixing too many fonts in the same spreadsheet or document. One or two should be enough.

Hint:

You can see a list of recent actions by clicking the arrow by the Undo button. You can then undo several actions at once. Use this feature with caution. It is safer to undo one action at a time so that you can see what is happening.

Task 3.12 — Use the undo feature

You can undo some of your actions, working backwards from the most recent.

Method

1　Click the Undo button on the Standard toolbar

If your last action was to change the font, then the font will change back.

Task 3.13 — Save, preview, print and close

Save your spreadsheet.
Preview the spreadsheet and print it on one sheet of paper.
There is no need to print the formulas again because they have not changed.
Close the spreadsheet.

Budget spreadsheet

You will make some alterations to the Budget spreadsheet. There are no new methods but there will be some reminders of the methods introduced for the Fruit spreadsheet.

Task 3.14 — Open the Budget spreadsheet

Click the Open button on the Standard toolbar.
Select the Budget.xls file and click Open.

Task 3.15 — Save the spreadsheet as Budget2

Click on the File menu and select Save As from the drop down list.
Key in the new name Budget2 into the dialogue box and click Save.

Task 3.16 — Edit cell contents

Go to cell B4 and change the amount of rent from 425 to 428.
Go to cell A5 and change the text to Council Tax.

Task 3.17 — Modify cell height and width

Widen columns A and B to width 12. Use the Format menu, Column, Width.
Give row 1 a height of 20. Use the Format menu, Row, Height.

Task 3.18 — Align cell contents

Go to cell B3 and align April to the right. Use the toolbar right align button.

Task 3.19 — Modify number formats

Select cells B4 to B11.
Format to currency with £ sign and 2 decimal places. Use the toolbar Currency button or the Format menu.

Task 3.20 — Modify text font, size and enhancements (bold, italic)

Select cells A4 to A11 and make them bold. Use the Bold button on the toolbar.
Go to cell B3 and make it bold.
Go to cell A1. Make it bold and font size 12.
Go to cell B11 and make it italic.

Hint:

Are you remembering to press Enter or click the green tick to fix the cell contents every time you key in data or edit old data? If you forget and leave a cell with a cursor in it, then you will find that many of the toolbar buttons and menu commands will not work. They will be greyed out. Enter the cell contents, then the buttons and menu commands will be available.

Task 3.21 — Use the undo feature

Click the Undo button on the toolbar so that cell B11 is no longer italic.

Task 3.22 — Save, print and close

Save the altered spreadsheet. Use the toolbar Save button.
Print the spreadsheet on one sheet of paper.
Close the spreadsheet.

→ Practise your skills 1 – Clothes invoice spreadsheet

You will make some changes to the Clothes invoice that you created in Section 2.

Instructions

1 Open the Clothes.xls spreadsheet file.
2 Save a copy of the file with the new name Clothes2.xls. Work on Clothes2.xls from now on.
3 Format cell A1 to bold and italic, size 16.
4 Format the headings in cells A5 to E5 to bold.
5 Format cells D10 and E10 to bold.
6 Format cells C6, C7 and the range E6 to E10 to show currency with a £ sign and 2 decimal places.
7 Change the width of columns A to E to 10.
8 Right align cells C5, D5 and E5.
9 Change the quantity of T-shirts to 6 and the quantity of Jeans to 3.
10 Check the final total. It should now be £112.69.
11 Save the altered spreadsheet.
12 Preview and print the spreadsheet on one sheet of paper.
13 Print the spreadsheet showing formulas on one sheet of paper.
14 Close the spreadsheet.

You will make some changes to the Stalls profit spreadsheet that you created in Section 2.

Instructions

1 Open the Stalls.xls spreadsheet file.
2 Save a copy of the file with the new name Stalls2.xls. Work on Stalls2.xls from now on.
3 Edit cell A1 to say **Summer Fete 2002**
4 Make cell A1 size 16 bold.
5 Make the following cells bold: A3, A8, A10, A14, A16, B8, B14, B16.
6 Format all cells containing amounts of money to show currency with £ sign and 2 decimal places.
7 Give columns A and B a width of 12.

	A	B	C
1	**Summer Fete 2002**		
2			
3	**Income**		
4	Cakes	£ 89.25	
5	Plants	£ 62.32	
6	Raffle	£ 96.75	
7	Tombola	£ 84.35	
8	**Total**	**£ 332.67**	
9			
10	**Expenses**		
11	Band	£ 57.75	
12	Prizes	£ 43.15	
13	Tickets	£ 6.35	
14	**Total**	**£ 107.25**	
15			
16	**Profit**	**£ 225.42**	
17			

Figure 3.10 Stalls spreadsheets with formatting

8 Change the income from the Raffle to £97.65.
9 Check that the profit is now £226.32.
10 Save the spreadsheet.
11 Print the spreadsheet on one sheet of paper.
12 Print the spreadsheet showing formulas on one sheet of paper.

→ **Check your knowledge**

1 You open an existing spreadsheet and make some changes. You want to save the new version so that it replaces the old version. What do you do?
2 You open an existing spreadsheet and make some changes. You want to save the new version but keep the old version too. What do you do?
3 A spreadsheet containing the budget for the year 2001 is called Budget2001. You want to make an altered version for the year 2002. Suggest a suitable name for the altered spreadsheet.
4 Changing the contents stored in a cell is called ...
5 Changing the appearance of a cell without changing the contents is called ...
6 Why is the appearance of a cell not always the same as the contents of the cell?

Figure 3.10 shows the design of a spreadsheet. Text and number data are shown in the cells. Some cells will contain formulas and these are shown with a box round them. They do not need boxes round them in the completed spreadsheet. There are notes telling you what formats should be used.

Instructions

1 Create a new spreadsheet file and save it with the name DIY Invoice.xls.

2 Prepare the spreadsheet as shown in the illustration.

3 Save the complete spreadsheet.

4 Print the spreadsheet showing the results on one sheet of paper.

5 Print the spreadsheet showing the formulas on one sheet of paper.

6 Close the spreadsheet.

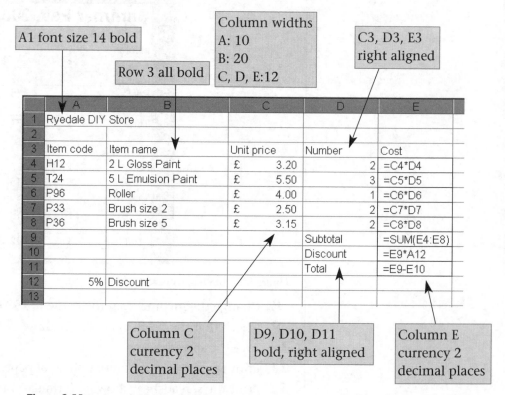

Figure 3.11 Design of the DIY spreadsheet

Section 4

Copying, inserting rows and choosing what to print

You will learn to

- Insert rows and columns into spreadsheets
- Delete rows and columns from spreadsheets
- Move and copy ranges of cells
- Replicate (copy) formulas
- Put borders round cells
- Produce hard copy of a spreadsheet and of selected areas of a spreadsheet on single sheets of paper

Budget spreadsheet

You will create a third version of the Budget spreadsheet and make some more alterations.

Task 4.1 — Open the Budget2 spreadsheet and save a new version

Open the existing spreadsheet Budget2.xls. It should look like Figure 4.1. It should also have your name in cell A13.

	A	B	C	D
1	Budget			
2				
3		April		
4	Rent	£ 428.00		
5	Council Tax	£ 64.00		
6	Electricity	£ 25.00		
7	Gas	£ 20.00		
8	Phone	£ 32.00		
9	Total	£ 569.00		
10				
11	Share	£ 284.50		
12				
13	Sue Ward			
14				
15				
16				
17				

Figure 4.1 The Budget2 spreadsheet

Save the spreadsheet as Budget3.xls. Work with Budget3.xls from now on.

Task 4.2 — Insert rows into a spreadsheet

Method

1   Go to cell A5.
2   Click on the Insert menu and select Rows from the drop down list.
3   Go to cell A9, which should now show the text Phone.
4   Click on the Insert menu and select Rows from the drop down list.

Hint:

Check formulas after inserting or deleting rows or columns to make sure that they still refer to the right cells.

You should now have two new empty rows, one between Rent and Council Tax, the other between Gas and Phone. Existing rows are renumbered as necessary.

Go to cell B11 which now contains the formula to find the total. Look at the formula bar. The formula has changed to =SUM(B4:B10) to include the two rows that were inserted.

Task 4.3 — Move a range of cells

You will move the entry for Electricity into the space below the entry for Gas.

Method

1   Select cells A7 and B7.
2   Click the Cut button on the Standard toolbar (Figure 4.2). Notice that a flashing dotted line, the marquee, surrounds your selected cells.
3   Go to cell A9.
4   Click the Paste button on the toolbar (Figure 4.2).
5   Check that the Electricity entry has moved to its new position.

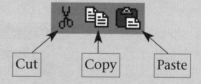

Cut   Copy   Paste

Figure 4.2 Cut, Copy and Paste buttons

Hint:

Drag and Drop is another method of moving cells.

Select the cell you want to move, then point the mouse to the edge of the cell. The mouse pointer should look like an arrow.

Hold down the left mouse button and drag the mouse to the new location. Release the mouse button.

Remember:

Save your spreadsheet often as you work.

Information: Cut and paste

Cut and Paste is a standard method of moving data or objects to a new location. It is available in most applications and in Windows itself.

When you cut an item, it is placed in a temporary storage area called the clipboard. When you paste, the item from the clipboard is inserted into your document.

Excel shares the clipboard with other Microsoft Office applications. Older versions of MS Office could hold only one item on the clipboard but the current version can hold up to 12 items. If you have several items on the clipboard then a window will appear giving you a choice of items to paste. The toolbar Paste button will paste the most recent item.

Task 4.4 — Copy a range of cells

You will copy the entry for Council Tax into row 5.

Method

1 Select cells A6 and B6.
2 Click the Copy button on the Standard toolbar (Figure 4.2). Notice that a flashing dotted line, the marquee, surrounds your selected cells.
3 Go to cell A5.
4 Click the Paste button on the toolbar.
5 Check that the Council Tax entry has been copied to its new position.

Information: Copy and paste

When you copy an item it remains in its original place, but a copy is stored on the clipboard. This copy can be pasted to a new location.

Hint:

You can use Drag and Drop to copy items. Hold down the Control key on the keyboard as you drag the item. Release the mouse button before you release the Control key. A copy of the item will go to the new location and the original will stay where it was.

Task 4.5 — Delete a row from a spreadsheet

Method

1 Select the whole of row 6 by clicking on its row number in the grey area to the left of the row. See Figure 4.3.

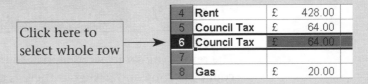

Click here to select whole row

4	Rent	£	428.00
5	Council Tax	£	64.00
6	Council Tax	£	64.00
7			
8	Gas	£	20.00

Figure 4.3 Selecting a row

2 Click on the Edit menu and select Delete from the drop down list.
3 The new row 6 should be an empty row and should already be selected.
4 Click on the Edit menu and select Delete from the drop down list.

Task 4.6 — Insert a column into a spreadsheet

Method

1 Go to cell B1 or any other cell in column B.
2 Click on the Insert menu and select Columns from the drop down list.

Hint:

Right click with the mouse, and you will see a pop-up menu with commands that apply to the object you clicked on.

If you right click on a spreadsheet cell, the menu will include cut, copy, paste.

If anything is available on the clipboard, insert, delete and format cells.

You can use pop-up menu commands as alternatives to the toolbar buttons or the main menu commands.

Task 4.7 Delete a column

Method

1. Select the whole of column B by clicking on the letter B above the column.
2. Click on the Edit menu and select Delete from the drop down list.

Task 4.8 Adding to the spreadsheet

You are going to add the expenses for three more months to the spreadsheet. You will learn a new copying method, but first there is some typing to do.

Make additional entries in cells so that your spreadsheet looks like Figure 4.4.

	A	B	C	D	E
1	**Budget**				
2					
3		April	May	June	July
4	Rent	£ 428.00			
5	Council Tax	£ 64.00			
6	Gas	£ 20.00			
7	Electricity	£ 25.00			
8	Phone	£ 32.00	£ 41.00	£ 62.00	£ 50.00
9	Total	£ 569.00			
10					
11	Share	£ 284.50			
12					

Figure 4.4 The altered Budget3 spreadsheet

Task 4.9 Copying cells using the fill handle

The rent is the same every month so the figure for April can be copied. You could use copy and paste but there is a quicker method of copying data along a row or down a column.

Method

1. Go to cell B4.
2. Point the mouse to a small dark square in the bottom right corner of the cell. This square is called the fill handle (Figure 4.5).

3		April	May	June	July
4	Rent	£ 428.00			
5	Council Tax	£ 64.00			

Fill handle

Figure 4.5 The fill handle

3. Check that the mouse pointer looks like a small black cross.
4. Hold down the left mouse button as you drag the mouse to cell E4.
5. Release the mouse button.

You can copy several cells at once using the fill handle.

Method

1. Select cells B5 to B7.
2. Point the mouse to the fill handle at the bottom right corner of cell B7.
3. Check that the mouse pointer looks like a small black cross.
4. Hold down the left mouse button as you drag the mouse to column E.
5. Release the mouse button.

Task 4.10   Replicate (copy) formulas

You can copy and paste formulas. You can also use the fill handle to copy formulas across rows or down columns.

Method

1. Go to cell B9, which contains a formula.
2. Point the mouse to the fill handle at the bottom right corner of cell B9.
3. Check that the mouse pointer looks like a small black cross.
4. Hold down the left mouse button as you drag the mouse to column E.
5. Release the mouse button.

Now check to see what has happened.

The formula in cell B9 is =SUM(B4:B8) to work out the total for April.
Go to cell C9 and look at the formula bar. The formula in C9 should be =SUM(C4:C8) to work out the total for May.
The formula in D9 should be =SUM(D4:D8)
The formula in E9 should be =SUM(E4:E8)

Use the fill handle to copy the formula in cell B11 across to cells C11, D11 and E11.

Remember:

Have you been saving regularly? Save now.

> ## Information: Relative and absolute cell references
>
> When you copy a formula it will adjust itself to suit its new position. It does this by altering the cell references it contains.
>
> Cell references are normally treated as identifying a position **relative** to the cell containing the formula. B9 contains the formula =SUM(B4:B8). B4:B8 are the 5 cells immediately above B9. Excel treats the formula as meaning 'add up the contents of the 5 cells above this cell'. When you copy the formula to C9, it will add the contents of the 5 cells above C9. The formula in C9 is changed to =SUM(C4:C8).
>
> Most of the time we want formulas to use relative positions and adjust their cell references when they are copied. Sometimes we want a cell reference to stay the same when it is copied so we make the reference **absolute**. Dollar signs are used to show that a reference is absolute. $B$4 is an absolute reference to cell B4. It will not change if a formula is copied to another cell.

Task 4.11 | Put borders round cells: Outline only

Method

1. Select cells AI to EII of your Budget3 spreadsheet.
2. Click on the Format menu and select Cells from the drop down list.
3. The Format Cells dialogue box opens. Click the Border tab (Figure 4.6).
4. Click the Outline button.
5. Click OK.

There is now a border round the range of cells AI to EII. The border does not show up clearly at the moment because of the gridlines.

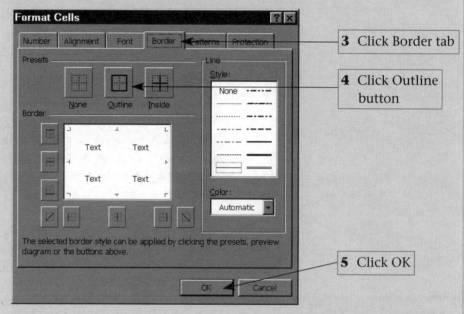

3 Click Border tab

4 Click Outline button

5 Click OK

Figure 4.6 The Format Cells dialogue box

Hint:

The Borders button on the toolbar shows the style of border you used most recently. You can use the button to put borders on cells. The arrow to the right of the button gives you a choice of border styles to apply.

Task 4.12 | Put borders round cells: Outline and inside

Method

1. Select cells A3 to E9.
2. Click on the Format menu and select Cells from the drop down list.
3. The Format Cells dialogue box opens. The Border tab should already be in front.
4. Click the Outline button and the Inside button.
5. Click OK.
6. Select cells AII to EII and use the same method to put outline and inside borders on this range of cells.

Information

Put in the borders last, after you have finished any copying, moving, inserting or deleting. Borders will be copied along with cell contents, and this may not be what you want.

Task 4.13	**Compare borders with gridlines for printing**

By default, gridlines are not shown in printouts. You learned in Section 2 how to show gridlines and headings in a printout. Gridlines can be useful for making a spreadsheet clearer, for example by showing which data belongs under which heading. Borders can be used for the same purpose, but they sometimes give a more attractive display because you can choose which cells have borders and which do not.

Method

1 Show the gridlines and headings for printing. Use the File menu, Page Setup, Sheet, click Gridlines, click Row and column headings to place ticks.
2 Click the Print Preview button to show the spreadsheet in Print Preview.
3 Look at the display to see how the gridlines are shown in the whole of the spreadsheet area. There is no need to print.
4 Hide the gridlines and headings for printing. Use the File menu, Page Setup, Sheet, click Gridlines, click Row and column headings to remove ticks.
5 Click the Print Preview button to show the spreadsheet in Print Preview.
6 Look at the display to see the borders that you placed round cells. There is no need to print.

Budget		April	May	June	July
Rent	£	428.00	£ 428.00	£ 428.00	£ 428.00
Council Tax	£	64.00	£ 64.00	£ 64.00	£ 64.00
Gas	£	20.00	£ 20.00	£ 20.00	£ 20.00
Electricity	£	25.00	£ 25.00	£ 25.00	£ 25.00
Phone	£	32.00	£ 41.00	£ 62.00	£ 50.00
Total	£	569.00	£ 578.00	£ 599.00	£ 587.00
Share	£	284.50	£ 289.00	£ 299.50	£ 293.50

Figure 4.7 The Budget3 spreadsheet without gridlines, showing borders

You will print the budget for April and May but not June and July.

Method

1 Select cells A1 to C13.
2 Click on the File menu and select Print from the drop down list.
3 The Print dialogue box appears (Figure 4.8).
4 Click the option button labelled Selection.
5 Click Preview to check what will be printed.
6 Click the Print button in the Preview window.

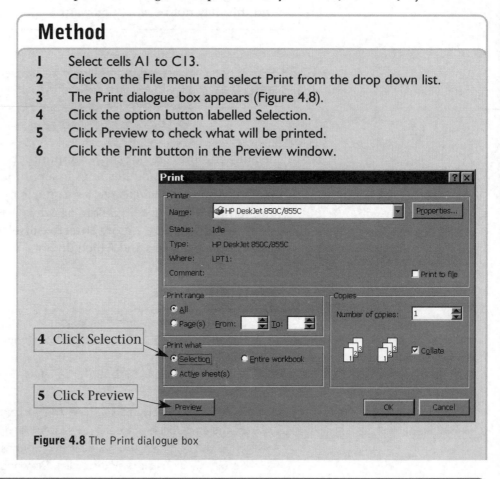

4 Click Selection

5 Click Preview

Figure 4.8 The Print dialogue box

Information: Printing a spreadsheet on a single sheet of paper

If possible, you should print a spreadsheet on one sheet of paper. It is more difficult to understand a spreadsheet if you have to line up several pages. Here are some suggestions.

Normal printouts showing results:

- You are creating fairly small spreadsheets, and they should fit on one sheet of paper for a normal printout.
- Change to landscape orientation of the paper if necessary.
- Choose sensible column widths that show all the data but do not take up too much unnecessary space.

Printouts showing formulas:

- Columns get wider as you change to Formula view, and this may make a spreadsheet too wide to fit on a sheet of paper.
- Use landscape orientation.
- It is not normally a good idea to reduce the column widths in Formula view. When you return to Normal view the columns get narrower and you would have to adjust them again.
- It may not be necessary to print the whole spreadsheet. You may be asked just to print the area with the formulas.
- If the spreadsheet will not quite fit on one page then use the 'Fit to page' option. Excel will temporarily reduce the size of everything on the sheet to make it fit.

The Budget spreadsheet is small enough to fit in landscape orientation when showing formulas, so Fit to page is not really necessary in this case. In order to demonstrate Fit to page, make sure that the spreadsheet is set to portrait orientation and is showing formulas.

Method

1   Check the Print Preview. You should find that the spreadsheet is too wide to fit on one sheet of paper when it is in portrait orientation and showing formulas. Close the Print Preview.
2   Click on the File menu and select Page Setup from the drop down list.
3   The Page tab should be in front. If not, click the Page tab (Figure 4.9).
4   Click in the Option button labelled Fit to. Keep the option of 1 page wide by 1 tall.
5   Click Print Preview.
6   Check the display, which should fit on one page, then Print.

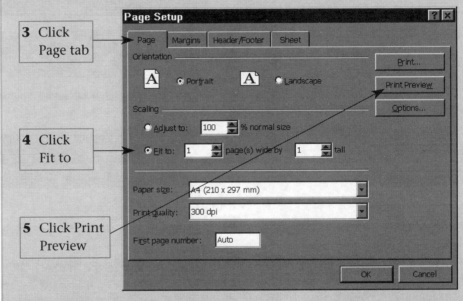

Figure 4.9 The Page Setup dialogue box

Information: Fit to page

If you choose the option of Fit to page, then Excel will change the size of the cells on the printout in order to fit them on the page. You can see this in Print Preview but the normal screen display will not be affected.

If you try to put too much on one page then this may make the text very small and difficult to read. Large spreadsheets may need to be printed on more than one page.

Task 4.16 Printing your name in a header

You have probably been typing your name into a spare spreadsheet cell in order to identify your printouts. Another way of printing your name is to put it in a header or a footer. A header is text that is printed at the top of every page of a document. A footer is printed at the bottom of every page.

Method

1 Click on the File menu and select Page Setup from the drop down list.
2 Click the Header/Footer tab (Figure 4.10).
3 Click Custom Header.

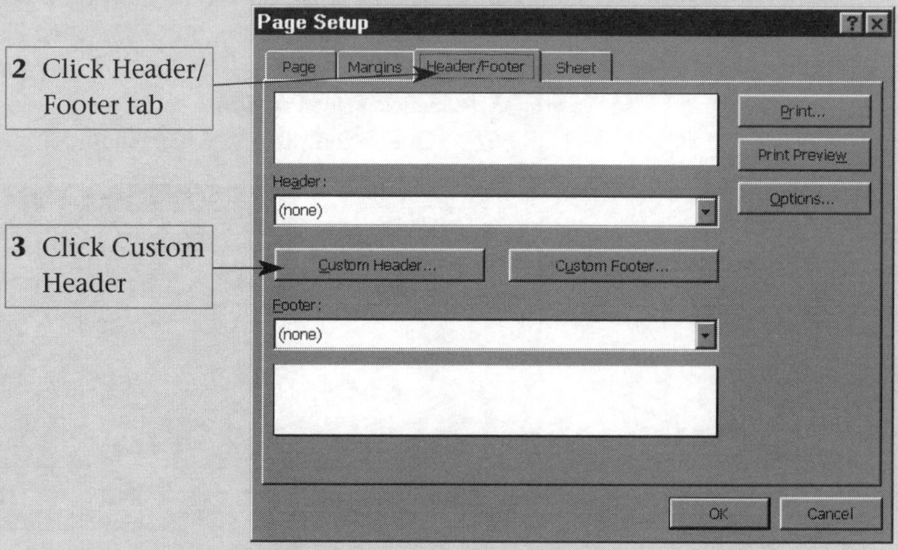

2 Click Header/ Footer tab

3 Click Custom Header

Page Setup

Page | Margins | Header/Footer | Sheet

Header:
(none)

Custom Header...   Custom Footer...

Footer:
(none)

Print...
Print Preview
Options...

OK   Cancel

Figure 4.10 Header and Footer dialogue

4 The Header dialogue box appears. It has three sections, left, centre and right.
5 Key in your name into the left section.
6 Click OK in the Header dialogue box, then click OK in the Page Setup dialogue box.
7 The header does not appear on the normal spreadsheet screen display, but you should see it at the top of the sheet when you next print preview or print.

Hint:

There is another way of getting to the Header and Footer dialogue. Click on the View menu and choose Header and Footer from the drop down list. This is the same as the method used in Microsoft Word.

Task 4.17 Save, print and close

1 Save the Budget3.xls spreadsheet again.
2 Print the results on one sheet of paper. There is no need to print the formulas again.
3 Close the spreadsheet.

→ Practise your skills 1 – Clothes invoice spreadsheet

Instructions

1 Open the Clothes2.xls spreadsheet that you created in Section 3.

2 Use Save As to save another copy of the spreadsheet. Call it Clothes3.xls.

3 Go to any cell in column A and insert a column to the left of column A.

4 Go to any cell in row 7 and insert a row above row 7.

5 Insert another row above the new row 7 so that you have two empty rows between T-shirt and Jeans.

6 Key in additional data in rows 7 and 8 so that your spreadsheet looks like Figure 4.11.

	A	B	C	D	E	F
1		*Clothes*				
2						
3			VAT rate	17.50%		
4						
5		**Code**	**Item**	**Price**	**Quantity**	**Cost**
6		M32	T shirt	£ 6.99	6	£ 41.94
7		M21	Socks	£ 1.50	5	
8		M35	Sweatshirt	£ 14.99	1	
9		M26	Jeans	£ 17.99	3	£ 53.97
10					Subtotal	£ 95.91
11					VAT	£ 16.78
12					**Total**	**£ 112.69**
13						

Figure 4.11 The altered Clothes3 spreadsheet

7 Use the fill handle to copy the formula from F6 down to cells F7 and F8.

8 Go to F7 and look at the formula bar to check that F7 contains the correct formula to multiply the price of socks by the quantity of socks.

9 Go to F8 and check that it contains the correct formula.

10 Check that the final total is now £139.12.

11 Select cells B1 to F12 and give them an outline border.

12 Select cells B5 to F9 and give them outline and inside borders.

13 Save the spreadsheet. (Have you been doing this regularly?)

14 Print the spreadsheet without gridlines.

15 Select cells B5 to F12 and print these cells only.

16 Print the whole spreadsheet, showing formulas, and showing gridlines and headings, on one sheet of paper.

→ Practise your skills 2 – Stalls spreadsheet

Instructions

1 Open the Stalls2.xls spreadsheet that you created in Section 3.
2 Save a new version of this spreadsheet as Stalls3.xls.
3 Insert a new row in the Income section between Cakes and Plants.
4 Cells A7 and B7 should now contain the text 'Raffle' and the number £97.65. Move the contents of these two cells to cells A5 and B5.
5 The Book stall had an income of £24.20. Enter the name and income of this stall into cells A7 and B7.
6 A local company kindly donated the prizes, so delete row 13. Make sure that you delete the complete row. Do not delete the cell contents and leave an empty row.
7 Adjust any cell formatting as necessary. All amounts of money should be displayed with a £ sign and 2 decimal places.
8 Check that the profit is now £293.67.
9 Select cells A3 to B9 and give them an outline border.
10 Select cells A11 to B14 and give them an outline border.
11 Select cells A16 to B16 and give them an outline border.
12 Print the complete spreadsheet without gridlines.
13 Print the income section, cells A3 to B9 only.
14 Print the complete spreadsheet, showing formulas, gridlines and row and column headings, on one sheet of paper.
15 Save again.
16 Optional – save a copy of the spreadsheet on a floppy disk.
17 Close the spreadsheet and close Excel.

The complete spreadsheet without gridlines is given in the Solutions section at the end of the book.

→ Practise your skills 3 – Items with VAT

The next spreadsheet looks very much like the Clothes spreadsheet, but there is an important difference. VAT is added to the cost of each individual item instead of to the total. This gives you a chance to practise using an absolute reference in a formula.

Instructions

	A	B	C	D	E	F
1	**Items with VAT**					
2						
3	Item	Unit price	No bought	Cost ex VAT	VAT	Cost with VAT
4	Toothpaste	£ 1.61	2			
5	Toothbrush	£ 1.69	2			
6	Tissues	£ 1.25	5			
7	Shampoo	£ 1.39	1			
8	Soap	£ 0.55	3			
9			Totals			
10						
11	VAT rate	17.50%				

Figure 4.12 VAT items spreadsheet

1. Create a new spreadsheet as shown, and save it as VAT items.xls.

2. Go to cell D4 and enter a formula to multiply the unit price by the number bought. Copy this formula down to cells D5, D6, D7 and D8.

3. Go to cell E4 and enter a formula to find the VAT. **=D4*B11** would give the right answer in cell E4, but it would not give the right answer when you copy it down to cell E5. In E5 it would change to =D5*B12. You want D4 to change to D5, but you do not want B11 to change. The reference to B11 should be absolute. The formula you need in cell E4 is =**D4*$B$11**.

4. Copy the formula from E4 down to cells E5, E6, E7 and E8.

5. Go to cell F4 and enter a formula to find the cost including VAT. Copy the formula down to cells F5, F6, F7 and F8.

6. In cell D9, enter a formula to find the total cost without VAT. The result should be £15.89.

7. Copy the formula from D9 across to E9 and F9. The VAT total should be £2.78. The total cost with VAT should be £18.67.

8. Make the column headings and the totals bold. Make the title bold and give it a larger font size.

9. Format all sums of money to currency with 2 decimal places.

10. Save the spreadsheet and print it on one sheet of paper.

11. Print the spreadsheet showing formulas, and showing gridlines and headings.

12. Insert a new row above the Tissues row.

13. Select cells A8 to F8, which should contain the Shampoo data, and move them into the new row.

14. Row 8 should now be empty. Delete it. You have swapped the positions of the Tissues and Shampoo entries.

15. Check that the totals are the same as before.

16. Go to any cell in column A and insert a new column. Give the new column a width of 2.33.

17. Give column H a width of 2.33.

18. Go to any cell in row 1 and insert a new row.

19. Select cells A1 to H13 and give them an outline border.

20. Select cells B2 to G12 and give them an outline border. You should now have a double border round the spreadsheet.

21. There is a rumour (untrue) that VAT is about to be changed to 20%. To see how this would affect the cost, change the VAT rate in cell C12 to 20%. You should find that the VAT total is now £3.18 and the total cost with VAT is now £19.07.

22. Save the spreadsheet.

23. Print the spreadsheet without gridlines so that your borders show clearly.

24. Close the spreadsheet.

→ Check your knowledge

1 When you insert a row, does it appear above or below the selected cell?

2 Cell C3 contains the number 6. You go to C3 and click the Copy button. You then go to C5 and click the Paste button. What does cell C3 contain now?

3 Cell C3 contains the number 6. You go to C3 and click the Cut button. You then go to C5 and click the Paste button. What does cell C3 contain now?

4 Where would you click the mouse to select a complete row?

5 What appears if you right click with the mouse?

6 Cell F5 contains the formula =SUM(F2:F4). You use the fill handle to copy this formula across to cells G5 and H5. What formula is now in H5?

7 Cell E12 contains the formula =C12*D12. You use the fill handle to copy this formula down to cells E13 and E14. What formula is now in E14?

8 Cell E12 contains the formula =$C$12*D12. You use the fill handle to copy this formula down to cells E13 and E14. What formula is now in E14?

9 Why is it a bad idea to make columns narrower in Formula view?

10 Which option should you select in the Print dialogue box if you want to print your chosen cells only?

Figure 4.13 shows the design of a spreadsheet. Text and number data are shown in the cells. Some cells will contain formulas and these are shown with a box round them. They do not need boxes round them in the completed spreadsheet. There are notes telling you what formats should be used.

Instructions

1 Create a new spreadsheet file and save it with the name Expense.xls.
2 Prepare the spreadsheet as shown in the illustration. Replicate the claim formula from E5 down the column to E8 (copy using fill handle).
3 Save the complete spreadsheet.
4 Print the spreadsheet showing the results on one sheet of paper.
5 Print cells E4 to E14 only, showing the formulas and showing gridlines and row and column headings.
6 Save the spreadsheet again as Expense2.xls.
7 Insert a row above row 6.
8 Move the data from row 8 to the new row 6.
9 Delete row 8.
10 Put borders (outline and inner) on cells A4 to E8 and A11 to E12 and D14 to E14.
11 Print the complete altered spreadsheet, without gridlines, showing results.
12 Save again then close the spreadsheet.

Remember:

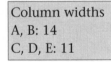

An integer is a whole number.

Column widths
A, B: 14
C, D, E: 11

Size 16 bold

A5 to A8 and A12: date format

A3, A4 to E4, A10, A11 to E11: bold headings

Miles in integer format

All money values shown 2 decimal places

D14 and E14 bold

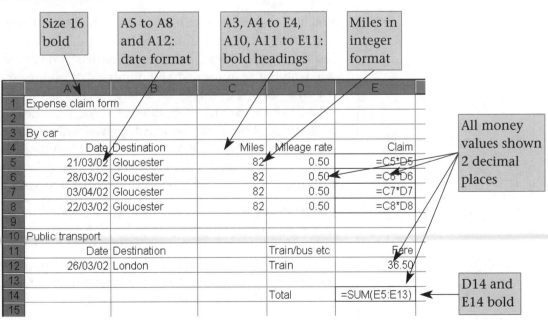

Figure 4.13 The Expense claim spreadsheet

	A	B	C	D	E
1	Expense claim form				
2					
3	By car				
4	Date	Destination	Miles	Mileage rate	Claim
5	21/03/02	Gloucester	82	0.50	=C5*D5
6	28/03/02	Gloucester	82	0.50	=C6*D6
7	03/04/02	Gloucester	82	0.50	=C7*D7
8	22/03/02	Gloucester	82	0.50	=C8*D8
9					
10	Public transport				
11	Date	Destination		Train/bus etc	Fare
12	26/03/02	London		Train	36.50
13					
14				Total	=SUM(E5:E13)
15					

Producing a spreadsheet from your own design

You will learn to

- Plan a spreadsheet layout for a given specification
- Choose suitable layouts and formats for data
- Choose suitable titles and labels
- Construct suitable formulas for calculated cells
- Identify the printout required for a given spreadsheet
- Use the AVERAGE, MAX and MIN functions

Information: Designing a spreadsheet

The specification

You have developed skills in using Excel and you can produce a spreadsheet by following a set of detailed instructions. Next you will learn how to design a spreadsheet to a specification. The specification for a spreadsheet is the information to tell you what is needed. You may be creating a spreadsheet for another person to use. We will call this person the 'user'. The user gives you the specification, and you follow it in order to produce a spreadsheet that is suitable for them.

The specification may just be in words, or you may be given an example on which you can base your design.

The design

You will design a spreadsheet on paper before you create it in Excel. You will draw the grid and write in any titles and headings. Clear headings are vital for letting people understand your spreadsheet. You will plan the areas for text and number data and maybe write the data into the cells. You will decide what formulas are needed to carry out calculations and write these into cells. You will also decide on formatting. Should numbers be displayed with decimal places and/or currency symbols? What font and size will you use? Should you highlight headings in bold? Will you need to make columns wider? All this information needs to be written on the design sheet.

It is tempting to start producing a spreadsheet using Excel without sketching a design on paper first. Try to avoid the temptation. It takes only a little time to sort out your ideas at the start, and it can save you a lot of time later. You are making small and simple spreadsheets now but one day you may be designing large and complex spreadsheets where good design is vital.

Your final assignment may include making a design on paper. If it does, then the design will be an important part of the marking scheme for the assignment.

Imports spreadsheet: The specification and design

You work for a company that imports fruit and vegetables from Europe, the USA and other countries all over the world. The company pays in the local currency of the country. The produce is sold in supermarkets. It is necessary to keep track of all the imports and convert the prices to pounds sterling.

Your colleague has a printout of a spreadsheet recording imports from the USA and giving the values in dollars and pounds. Your colleague needs a similar spreadsheet to record imports from European Union countries, giving the values in euros and pounds. The original spreadsheet is shown in Figure 5.1.

The exchange rate from euros to pounds is 0.612, and the imports come from different countries rather than different states.

Imports from USA			
Exchange rate	$ to £	0.696	
State	Product	Value $	Value £
California	oranges	2000.00	1392.00
Kansas	potatoes	1000.00	696.00
Kansas	sweetcorn	3000.00	2088.00
	Total	6000.00	4176.00

Figure 5.1 Example import spreadsheet

Task 5.2 Plan the spreadsheet layout on paper with titles and labels

Method

Rule a grid on paper and write in the titles and labels for the new spreadsheet in pen or pencil. It should look rather like Figure 5.2.

	A	B	C	D
1	Imports from European Union countries			
2				
3	Exchange rate	€ to £	0.612	
4				
5	Country	Product	Value €	Value £
6				
7				
8				
9				
10		Total		

Figure 5.2 Initial design of EU import spreadsheet

Method

1   Decide on suitable column widths and make a note of this on your design. Column A could have width 13 and the other columns could have width 10.

2   Choose a font and size for the main part of the spreadsheet and write it in. Arial size 10 is commonly used.

3   Choose a font and size for the title. Write this on your plan. I have decided to keep Arial font but make it size 12 and bold.

4   Headings could be made bold, so write this in.

5   Cells C6 to D10 will contain the euro and pound values. These should be formatted to number with 2 decimal places. Write it in.

By now your plan should look rather like Figure 5.3.

	A	B	C	D
1	Imports from European Union countries			
2				
3	Exchange rate	€ to £	0.612	
4				
5	Country	Product	Value €	Value £
6				
7				
8				
9				
10		Total		

Title Arial size 12 bold

Headings bold
A5 to D5 and B10

Number, 2 decimal places in C6 to D10

Widths
A: 13
B, C, D: 10

Main font Arial size 10

Figure 5.3 Design with formats

1   Cell D6 will need a formula to multiply the value in euros by the exchange rate. =C6*C3 looks promising.
There may be a problem though, when the formula is copied down to cells D7 and D8.
D7 is one cell below D6, so all the references in the copied formula will be one cell lower: =C7*C4. We want C6 to change to C7, but we want C3 to stay the same every time. It needs an absolute reference. =C6*$C$3 is the formula to put in cell D6. It can be copied to D7 and D8.

2   Cell C10 needs a SUM function to add up the euro values =SUM(C6:C9). Cell D10 also needs a SUM function, but this can be copied from C10.

3   Write the formulas into their cells and draw a box round cells with formulas. This is just to emphasise the fact that they contain formulas. It does not mean that the cells should have outlines in the finished spreadsheet.

Your design could now look like Figure 5.4.

	A	B	C	D
1	Imports from European Union countries			
2				
3	Exchange rate	€ to £	0.612	
4				
5	Country	Product	Value €	Value £
6				=C6*$C$3
7				
8				copy
9				▼
10		Total	=SUM(C6:C9)	copy ▶

Title Arial size 12 bold

Headings bold
A5 to D5 and B10

Number, 2 decimal places in C6 to D10

Widths
A: 13
B, C, D: 10

Main font Arial size 10

Figure 5.4 Design of import spreadsheet with formulas

Information: Cell references in formulas

The formula to find the value in pounds could have been =C6*0.612. This would have given the right answer. It could have been copied without any problem. Instead of doing this, we put the value 0.612 in a cell, and used a reference to the cell in the formula. Why? Because it makes the spreadsheet much easier to update if the exchange rate changes. It is easy to change the value in a cell, but harder to change several formulas. It is good practice to use cell references in formulas and not use actual numbers.

Task 5.5   Identify printouts needed

Two printouts will be needed: one of the whole spreadsheet showing the results and one showing the formulas with gridlines and row/column headings.

Imports spreadsheet: Create the spreadsheet to the design

Task 5.6   Create the spreadsheet and enter data

Method

1   Start Excel with a new spreadsheet.
2   Enter the title and labels as shown in your design. To key in the euro symbol, hold down the Alt Gr key and press 4. If nothing happens then your computer system does not support the euro symbol. Just key in the word euro instead.
3   Enter the data.

Country	Product	Value €
Spain	oranges	1000.00
Spain	potatoes	2000.00
France	apples	500.00

Table 5.1 Imports from EU countries

Task 5.7 · Enter and test formulas

Method

1 Key in the formula in cell D6 as shown in your design.
2 Use the fill handle to replicate (copy) the formula down to D8.
3 Key in the formula in cell C10 as shown in your design.
4 Use the fill handle to replicate the formula to cell D10.
5 Work out the results yourself and compare your answers with the spreadsheet results. You can use a calculator or you can work out the answers in your head or on paper. You are checking that the spreadsheet formulas have been entered correctly to give the right results.
6 If your own results are not the same as the spreadsheet results then there is a mistake either in the formula or in your own calculation. Check again carefully. Correct the formula if it is wrong.

Hint:

Put test data in the cells, using numbers chosen to make the calculations easy for you to do yourself. After you have checked the formulas, you can put in the real data.

Task 5.8 · Apply formatting and make any adjustments

Method

1 Adjust the column width. Set the font and font size. Set the numbers to show 2 decimal places. Make the headings bold. Do all this following the notes on your design sheet. Your spreadsheet should look something like Figure 5.5.

	A	B	C	D
1	**Imports from European Union countries**			
2				
3	Exchange rate	€ to £	0.612	
4				
5	**Country**	**Product**	**Value €**	**Value £**
6	Spain	oranges	1000.00	612.00
7	Spain	potatoes	2000.00	1224.00
8	France	apples	500.00	306.00
9				
10		**Total**	3500.00	2142.00
11				

Figure 5.5 The Imports spreadsheet

2 Make any adjustments you need and write down what you did. You might right align the labels in cells C5 and C6. There is almost always something to change at this stage.

Hint:

You are not expected to make a perfect design first time. It is normal to make some changes when you have created the actual spreadsheet. It is important that you record these changes.

Task 5.9 — Save, print and close

Method

1 Save your spreadsheet as **EU imports**.xls.
2 Preview and print the whole spreadsheet showing the results. As you have not put borders round cells, it would be a good idea to show gridlines.
3 Print the spreadsheet on one sheet of paper, showing formulas. Show gridlines and row and column headings.
4 Close the spreadsheet.

Waste disposal spreadsheet: The specification and design

Task 5.10 — Study the specification

Your boss says to you: 'I need a spreadsheet that shows what our three local district councils did with the waste they collected. I have the figures in tonnes for landfill, incineration, recycling and composting for each council (Table 5.2). I want to know the total waste handled by each council and I want the average figures for each disposal method. You might be able to adapt the spreadsheet that shows the spending for each council (Figure 5.6). I think the layout should be similar. I don't like the font but I do like the boxes round the cells. I think the headings should be highlighted, and could the word Average be moved to the right?'

	East Melford	West Melford	South Melford
Landfill	48800	25000	52000
Incineration	8000	0	12000
Recycled	2100	2000	1200
Composted	1800	1400	500

Table 5.2 Waste disposal data for Melford

```
                        District Council Spending

Thousands of pounds
                     East Melford  West Melford  South Melford  Average
Environmental             3504          1020          3300        2608
Planning                  2444          1540          2090        2025
Leisure and tourism       2268          2100          2300        2223
Refuse collection         1378          1800          1490        1556
Total                     9594          6460          9180
```

Figure 5.6 Example spreadsheet – District Council spending

Task 5.11 — Plan the spreadsheet layout on paper with titles and labels

Method

Rule a grid on paper and write in the titles and labels for the new spreadsheet. You already have the new figures so put these in too. Your design should look rather like Figure 5.7.

	A	B	C	D	E
1		District Council Waste Disposal			
2					
3	Tonnes				
4		East Melford	West Melford	South Melford	Average
5	Landfill	48800	25000	52000	
6	Incineration	8000	0	12000	
7	Recycled	2100	2000	1200	
8	Composted	1800	1400	500	
9	Total				

Figure 5.7 First design for waste disposal spreadsheet

Task 5.12 — Choose formats

Write notes on your design to show the formats. Include the following:

- Main font Arial size 10.
- Heading font. Choose a font that stands out well. You can choose from the fonts available to you.
- Column widths. I suggest width 14 for all columns.
- Headings in B4 to E4 and A5 to A9 should be bold.
- Align headings in B4 to E4 to the right.
- You need not use borders. If you wish to do so, you could place them round cells as follows: A1 to E1, A4 to E9, A4 to A9, E4 to E9, A9 to E9.

Task 5.13 — Construct formulas

There are two kinds of calculation needed. One is to find the totals of the columns, and the other is to find the average of each row. You will meet a new function that finds an average.

Method

1   In cell B9 of your design, write in a formula that uses the SUM function to add cells B5 to B8.

2   This formula can be replicated (copied) to cells C9 and D9.

3   In cell E5 you need a formula to find the average of the numbers in cells B5 to D5. To find the average of 3 numbers you add up the numbers then divide by 3. You could use the formula =SUM(B5:D5)/3. A better method is to use the AVERAGE function =AVERAGE(B5:D5). Write this into cell E5.

4   This formula can be replicated to cells E6, E7 and E8.

Information: Functions

Excel has many functions to carry out special calculations. Functions are used inside formulas. SUM is used most often. AVERAGE finds the average of the values in a range of cells. MAX, short for maximum, finds the largest value in a range of cells, e.g. =MAX(B5:D5) would give 52000 in the waste spreadsheet. MIN, short for minimum, finds the smallest value in a range of cells, e.g. =MIN(B5:D5) would give 25000 in the waste spreadsheet. There are hundreds of other functions for specialised financial, mathematical, statistical and other calculations. You may meet some of them if you take a more advanced spreadsheet course.

Task 5.14 — Identify printouts needed

The boss has not said anything special about printouts so you need the usual two: a printout of results and a printout of formulas. The formula printout should show gridlines and row/column headings. The results printout may not need gridlines if you have chosen to put borders round cells. Write a note on your design sheet to say what printouts you need.

Waste disposal spreadsheet: Create the spreadsheet to the design

Task 5.15 — Create the spreadsheet and enter data

Method

1   Start Excel with a new spreadsheet.
2   Enter the title and labels and data as shown in your design.

Task 5.16 — Enter and test formulas

Method

1   Key in the formula in cell B6 as shown in your design.
2   Use the fill handle to replicate (copy) the formula across to D9.
3   Key in the formula in cell E5 as shown in your design.
4   Use the fill handle to replicate the formula down to cell E8.
5   Work out the results yourself and compare your answers with the spreadsheet results. You can use a calculator or you can work out the answers in your head or on paper. Make sure that your own answers are the same as the spreadsheet results. If not, there may be a mistake in a formula. It is a good idea to use simple test data when checking formulas, then put in the real data when you know that the formulas are correct.

Task 5.17 — Apply formatting and make any adjustments

1 Put in all the formatting, following the notes on your design sheet. Your spreadsheet in Print Preview could look something like Figure 5.8. It will look a bit different if you have chosen to print gridlines, but the numbers should be the same.

District Council Waste Disposal

Tonnes

	East Melford	West Melford	South Melford	Average
Landfill	48800	25000	52000	41933
Incineration	8000	0	12000	6667
Recycled	2100	2000	1200	1767
Composted	1800	1400	500	1233
Total	60700	28400	65700	

Figure 5.8 Council Waste spreadsheet

2 Do you want to make any changes? You might decide to make Tonnes bold, or change the column widths a little. Make the changes and write down everything you do.

Task 5.18 — Save, print and close

Method

1 Save the spreadsheet with the name Council Waste.xls.
2 Print the spreadsheet showing the results.
3 Print the formulas showing gridlines and row/column headings.
4 Close the spreadsheet.

Information: Planning formulas

You know how to add, subtract, multiply and divide in formulas using the four arithmetic operators +, −, * and /, e.g. =B4+B5, =B4−B5, =B4*B5, =B4/B5. You can combine operators in the same formula, e.g. =B4+B5−B6, =B4*B5+B6. The normal rules of arithmetic apply to spreadsheet formulas:

* Calculations in brackets are carried out first.
* Multiplying and dividing are carried out next.
* Adding and subtracting are carried out last.

10+2*3 gives 16 because you multiply 2*3 first, giving 6, then add 10+6. (10+2)*3 gives 36 because you take the brackets first. 10+2 gives 12, then 12*3 gives 36.

In school you may have learned BODMAS. This is a way of remembering the order of carrying out calculations. Brackets, Of, Divide, Multiply, Add, Subtract.

You also know the SUM, MAX, MIN and AVERAGE functions. Remember that SUM is just for adding. You don't use it for other kinds of calculations.

You may be asked to set up formulas with two arithmetic operators. It is possible to use very complicated formulas with many operators, but it is not a good idea. People are more likely to make mistakes when planning and keying in complicated formulas. It is better to use several simple formulas in different cells than one complicated formula. Good design keeps the spreadsheet as simple as possible.

Task 5.19 Use a formula combining * and − operators

Customers are allowed a discount on the cost of goods and you need to work out how much the customers should pay. First you will do this in two stages using simple formulas, then you will combine the calculations on one formula.

Method

1 Create a spreadsheet as shown in Figure 5.9.

	A	B	C	D
1	Cost	Discount rate	Discount	To Pay
2	£ 274.00	2%		

Figure 5.9 Discount spreadsheet with 4 columns

2 Discount is Cost * Discount rate, so go to cell C2 and enter the formula =A2*B2.
3 To Pay is Cost − Discount, so go to cell D2 and enter the formula =A2−C2.
4 Check that the Discount is £5.48 and To Pay is £268.52.
5 Create a second spreadsheet as shown in Figure 5.10.

	A	B	C
1	Cost	Discount rate	To Pay
2	£ 274.00	2%	

Figure 5.10 Discount spreadsheet with 3 columns

6 Combining the two calculations, To Pay is Cost − Cost * Discount Rate. The multiplying will be carried out before the subtracting. Go to cell C2 and enter the formula =A2−A2*B2.
7 Check that the result To Pay is £268.52 as it was before.
8 Close the spreadsheets. There is no need to save or print them.

Task 5.20 Use a formula combining * and + operators

A club buys a set of printed T-shirts for resale to its members. The club wants to raise funds so it adds a markup to the cost of each T-shirt to give the selling price.

Method

1   Create a spreadsheet as shown in Figure 5.11.

	A	B	C
1	Cost price	markup	selling price
2	£ 3.00	5%	

Figure 5.11 Spreadsheet

2   To find out how much must be added to the cost price, you work out Cost price * markup. You then add this amount to the cost price. The full formula for the selling price is therefore Cost price + Cost price*markup. Go to cell C2 and enter the formula =A2+A2*B2.

3   Check that the result for the selling price is £3.15.

4   Close the spreadsheet. There is no need to save or print it.

Information: Paper sizes

Paper size A4 is most commonly used for computer printouts in the UK. A4 paper is 29.7 cm by 21 cm. A5 is half the size of A4 at 21 cm by 14.9 cm. Many of your spreadsheets fit in the top half of a sheet of A4 paper in portrait orientation. You could have printed them using A5 paper in landscape orientation.

A4 landscape

A4 portrait

A5 landscape

Figure 5.12 A4 and A5 paper

When you design a spreadsheet, you may be asked what size and orientation of paper should be used for printing. You can specify A4 portrait, A4 landscape or A5 landscape as appropriate. It may be possible to set up your printer to take A5 or other sizes of paper. This will depend on the make and model. In practice, you may be doing all your printing on A4 paper.

→ Practise your skills 1 – Police authority spending

Past and planned spending by the local police authority is as follows:

	2000/01 £ thousands	2001/02 £ thousands	2002/03 £ thousands
Police pay	100377	120109	120338
Pensions	18390	19804	21765
Civilian staff	32670	41566	50927
Training	1993	2018	2061
Other	48328	49918	58201

Table 5.3 Spending by police authority

Instructions

1 Design a spreadsheet on paper to display these figures. There should be a title at the top. There should be a row at the bottom showing the total spending for each year.

2 Decide on the column widths and formatting you will use. Write these on your design.

3 Write in a formula to find the total for the year 2000/01. You should be able to copy this formula for the other years.

4 Start Excel and create a spreadsheet exactly according to your design. Call it Police spending.xls.

5 Check the formulas. It is a good idea to use simple numbers for checking.

6 Print the spreadsheet.

7 On the printout, write down any changes you need to improve the appearance of the spreadsheet.

8 Make the changes then print the spreadsheet again.

9 Print the formulas, showing gridlines and row/column headings.

→ Practise your skills 2 – Sharing a meal

Four people share a meal. They agree to split the cost equally between them. You are going to design and create a spreadsheet to work out the total cost and each person's share. You could base the design on the Budget spreadsheet shown in Figure 4.1 of Section 4. The data for the new spreadsheet is as follows:

Chicken in black bean sauce	5.20
Sweet and sour pork	5.25
Beef with mushroom	5.75
Stir fried vegetables	5.00
Fried rice for four	6.00

Table 5.4 Sharing the cost of a meal

Instructions

1 Design a spreadsheet on paper to display these figures. There should be a title at the top. There should be a row at the bottom showing the total cost of the meal and another row showing the share to be paid by each person.

2 Decide on the column widths and formatting you will use. Write these on your design.

3 Write in a formula to find the total. Write in a formula to find the share. (Total divided by 4.)

4 Start Excel and create a spreadsheet exactly according to your design. Call it Meal.xls.

5 Check the formulas.

6 Print the spreadsheet.

7 On the printout, write down any changes you need to improve the appearance of the spreadsheet.

8 Make the changes then print the spreadsheet again.

9 Print only the area of cells containing formulas. Show formulas, gridlines and row/column headings.

→ Practise your skills 3 – Temperatures

You are asked to create a spreadsheet to display temperature measurements taken four times a day over a seven-day period. The maximum, minimum and average temperatures are required for each day and for the whole week. Measurements are as follows.

Time	Sun	Mon	Tues	Wed	Thurs	Fri	Sat
02:00	5	4	−1	0	3	5	2
08:00	9	8	8	10	12	15	10
14:00	20	22	18	16	20	28	22
20:00	14	15	12	11	15	17	15

Table 5.5 Daily temperature readings

Instructions

1 Design a spreadsheet on paper to display these figures. There should be a title at the top. There should be rows at the bottom showing the maximum value, the minimum value and the average value for each day. There should be additional cells showing the maximum, minimum and average values for the whole week.

2 Decide on the column widths and formatting you will use. Write these on your design. Average values should be shown to 2 decimal places. All other numbers should be shown as integers.

3 Write in the necessary formulas. Use the MAX, MIN and AVERAGE functions. Make a note of any places where you may be able to replicate (copy) formulas.

4 Start Excel and create a spreadsheet exactly according to your design. Call it Temperatures.xls.

5 Check the formulas.

6 Print the spreadsheet.

7 On the printout, write down any changes you need to improve the appearance of the spreadsheet.

8 Make the changes then print the spreadsheet again.

9 Print only the area of cells containing formulas. Show formulas, gridlines and row/column headings.

→ Practise your skills 4 – T-shirts

Try to do this skills practice without looking back at Task 5.20.

A club buys various items printed with the club logo to resell to members. The club adds a markup to the cost of each item to give the selling price. You are asked to create a spreadsheet to work out the selling price for each item.

Item	Cost price	Markup
T-shirt	£3.00	5%
Sweatshirt	£11.00	2%
Cap	£6.00	10%
Bag	£8.00	4%

Table 5.6 Sales of printed items

Instructions

1 Design a spreadsheet on paper to display these figures. There should be a title at the top. There should an additional column on the right, headed Selling Price.

2 Decide on the column widths and formatting you will use. Decide on the alignment of headings or data. Write these on your design. Cost price and selling price should be shown to 2 decimal places.

3 Write in the necessary formula to work out the selling price of a T-shirt. Make a note of any places where you may be able to replicate (copy) formulas.

4 Start Excel and create a spreadsheet exactly according to your design. Call it Tshirts.xls.

5 Check the formula results using a calculator or pen and paper.

6 Print the spreadsheet.

7 On the printout, write down any changes you need to improve the appearance of the spreadsheet.

8 Make the changes then print the spreadsheet again. Show gridlines unless you have chosen to put borders round cells.

9 Print only the area of cells containing formulas. Show formulas, gridlines and row/column headings.

→ Check your knowledge

For questions 1–5, assume that cell B1 contains the value 4, B2 contains the value 10 and B3 contains the value 5.

1 What is the result given by the formula =B2−B3?

2 What is the result given by the formula =B1*B2?

3 What is the result given by the formula =B1+B2*B3?

4 What is the result given by the formula =(B1+B2)*B3?

5 What is the result given by the formula =SUM(B1:B3)?

6 Why is it better to use several simple formulas than one complicated formula?

Practice assignments

In order to achieve the Level 1 spreadsheet qualification, you need to take and pass one assignment. There are Pass, Credit and Distinction grades available. Your tutor will give you the real assignment when you and your tutor agree that you are ready.

You will be producing written and printed work. Your tutor will also need to check your saved files. Your tutor will tell you where you should save your files. This may be in a special network area or it may be on a floppy disk.

Practice assignment 1: SavePlus

Read all the instructions carefully before starting work.

You must, at all times, observe all relevant health and safety precautions.

Time allowed: 1½ hours

Introduction

This assignment is broken down into 2 parts:

1 Task A asks you to produce a spreadsheet specification from the user description, and to identify labelling and formatting.

2 Task B asks you to create a spreadsheet with test data given.

> ### Scenario
> You have to design and produce a spreadsheet to calculate the wages to be paid to employees of SavePlus Supermarkets.
>
> ### MultiMarkets
>
> Part time employees' wages
> Week starting: 09/09/02
>
> | Name | Hours worked Mon-Fri | Sat | Sun | Total hours | Hourly rate | Pay for week |
> |------|------|-----|-----|-------|------|------|
> | Byers D | 15 | 0 | 0 | 15 | £ 4.00 | £ 60.00 |
> | Dawson M | 8 | 6 | 6 | 20 | £ 5.00 | £ 100.00 |
> | Hussein A | 12 | 4 | 4 | 20 | £ 5.00 | £ 100.00 |
> | O'Driscoll P | 25 | 0 | 0 | 25 | £ 6.00 | £ 150.00 |
> | Sullivan K | 30 | 0 | 0 | 30 | £ 6.00 | £ 180.00 |
> | Varju P | 15 | 0 | 0 | 15 | £ 6.00 | £ 90.00 |
> | Wilcox G | 10 | 6 | 4 | 20 | £ 6.00 | £ 120.00 |
> | | | | | | Total: | £ 800.00 |
>
> **Figure 6.1** Sample spreadsheet – MultiMarkets
>
> Your boss has a copy of a spreadsheet used by MultiMarkets, and gives it to you with some comments. 'Base your design on this spreadsheet, but make some changes. I don't like the font. Use Arial or a similar font for the main part of the form, but use another font for the company name. The headings should be highlighted. Some of the

> headings could be better justified too. The columns and rows need to be clear so can you either print the gridlines or else put borders round the cells like the example? Check that the spreadsheet works with some simple numbers first as this one does, and then print me a real spreadsheet from the data you are given.'

Task A Design

1 Inspect the sample carefully and study your boss's comments.

2 Hand-sketch the spreadsheet to be created following your boss's preferences where possible. Draw boxes round any areas containing formulas.

3 Mark in any changes from the default values of:
- column width and row height
- font sizes
- fonts
- highlighting that you will use
- justification.

Mark any places where special precautions have to be taken to keep zeros visible by setting the number of decimal places to display.

4 Mark on the design your column and row numbers and then add:
- a sample of the formula used to calculate Total hours
- a sample of the formula used to calculate Pay for Week
- the formula used to calculate the Total.

5 Decide and mark on the design: the paper size and orientation required for printing this spreadsheet. Keep the design sheet for later comparison.

Task B

1 Start up the spreadsheet software and start a new spreadsheet.

2 Add the headings, labels and enter the test data as follows:

Company = SavePlus
Week starting = 30/9/2002

Name	Hours worked			Total hours	Hourly rate
	Mon-Fri	Sat	Sun		
Evans E	22	0	0		£ 4.25
Jones H	17	6	6		£ 5.30
Jones T	8	4	4		£ 5.30
Owen G	10	5	4		£ 5.75
Price C	25	0	0		£ 5.75
Rees J	30	0	0		£ 6.20
Thomas S	10	6	5		£ 5.75

Table 6.1 Data for SavePlus spreadsheet

3 Add the formulas that you have specified.

Copy/replicate the Total hours formula and the Pay for Week formula into each row.

Check that the Total and other calculations are correct.

4 Adjust the format of the various parts of the spreadsheet so that it matches your design.

5 Print out a copy of the spreadsheet on a single sheet of paper and mark it Printout1

6 Hand-write on Printout1 any further modifications that you needed to make to implement the design. Correct any errors.

7 Save your edited sheet with an appropriate filename, and with an appropriate file extension. Write this filename clearly on Printout1.

8 Put in your own surname and initial as the first employee instead of Evans E and set your hourly rate to £6.20. Put in today's date for Week starting.

9 Print out a copy of the spreadsheet on a single sheet of paper and mark it Printout2

10 Swap the data from the first and second rows of the list of employees by using the move, insert, delete functions. Print out a copy of the spreadsheet on a single sheet of paper and mark it Printout3.

11 Set the spreadsheet to print out formulas and print out just the area containing formulas, with gridlines showing and rows and columns labelled. Mark it as Printout4.

12 Save a new version of your edited sheet. Write the filename clearly on Printout4.

13 Close down the spreadsheet software.

Note:
- At the conclusion of this assignment, hand all paperwork and disks to the test supervisor.
- Ensure that your name is on the disk (if using a floppy disk) and all documentation.
- If the assignment is taken over more than one period, all floppy disks and paperwork must be returned to the test supervisor at the end of each sitting.

Practice assignment 2: Bonus payments

Candidates are advised to read all instructions carefully before starting work and to check with your assessor, if necessary, to ensure that you have fully understood what is required.

You must, at all times, observe all relevant health and safety precautions.

Time allowed: 1½ hours

Introduction

This assignment is in 2 parts:

1   Task A requires candidates to produce a spreadsheet specification from the user description, to identify labelling and formatting, then to create the spreadsheet.

2   Task B requires candidates to modify the spreadsheet.

Scenario

Your firm pays sales people a bonus based on the value of the sales they have made. You are asked to design and create a spreadsheet to work out how much each sales person should be paid. The bonus is worked out by multiplying the sales figure by the bonus rate. The bonus then has to be added to the basic pay. Names, sales figures and bonus rates and basic pay are as follows:

Name: N James, Sales: £43200, Bonus rate: 0.20%, Basic pay: £1,200.00
Name: D Lee, Sales: £58360, Bonus rate: 0.50%, Basic pay: £1,200.00
Name: W Matthews, Sales: £20906, Bonus rate: 0.50%, Basic pay: £1,350.00
Name: G Rogers, Sales: £62400, Bonus rate: 0.20%, Basic pay: £1,350.00
Name: M Yau, Sales: £53180, Bonus rate: 0.20%, Basic pay: £1,400.00

Task A Design

1   Read the information in the scenario.

2   Sketch a plan of your spreadsheet on paper. Put in a suitable title and column headings. Add the data.

3   Write in the formats. The title should be a suitable font and size to show up well. The column headings should be bold. Use appropriate justification to left, right or centre. Sales figures should be shown as currency with no decimal places. Basic pay and pay with bonus should be currency with 2 decimal places. Indicate clearly which cells contain text and which contain numbers.

4   Write in a sample of the formula you will use to calculate the amount of pay including the bonus for one person. Show how you can replicate this formula to calculate the pay of the other sales people.

5   Write in a formula to find the total paid to all the sales people.

6   Start up the Spreadsheet software and start a new spreadsheet.

7   Create the spreadsheet according to your design. Enter the title, column headings and data.

8 Add the formulas to calculate the pay with bonus for each sales person, and to calculate the total.

9 Format spreadsheet cells according to your design.

10 Save your spreadsheet as BONUS1.

11 Print out the spreadsheet in portrait orientation and write BONUS1 on the printout.

12 Print out the spreadsheet on one sheet of paper in landscape orientation showing the formulas and showing gridlines and row and column headings. Write BONUS1 formulas on the printout.

Task B

Make the following changes to the spreadsheet.

1 Copy all the headings and data and formulas, but not the title, to a new position further down the spreadsheet, so that you have two copies of the same data.

2 In the lower section of the spreadsheet, replace the old sales figures with the current sales figures which are:
N James: £ 38,750, D Lee: £ 51,600, W Matthews: £ 29,603,
G Rogers: £ 55,400, M Yau: £ 48,000

3 In the lower section of the spreadsheet, insert a row between W Matthews and G Rogers. Enter the pay details for P Nolan who had sales figures of £31,947, a bonus rate of 0.20% and a basic pay of £1400.

4 Replicate a formula to find the pay with bonus for P Nolan.

5 In the lower section of the spreadsheet, add an extra column heading to the right: Deductions.

6 Calculate a deduction of 20% of the pay with bonus for each person.

7 Find the total of the deductions.

8 Save your spreadsheet as BONUS2.

9 Print out only the lower section of your spreadsheet and write BONUS2 on your printout.

10 In the lower section of the spreadsheet, delete the row containing the details for D Lee, who has left the company.

11 Save your spreadsheet as BONUS3.

12 Print out the whole spreadsheet. Write BONUS3 on the printout.

13 Close down the spreadsheet software.

Note:
- At the conclusion of this assignment, hand all paperwork and disks to the test supervisor.
- Ensure that your name is on the disk (if using a floppy disk) and all documentation.
- If the assignment is taken over more than one period, all floppy disks and paperwork must be returned to the test supervisor at the end of each sitting.

Practice assignment 3: Savings account

Candidates are advised to read all instructions carefully before starting work and to check with your assessor, if necessary, to ensure that you have fully understood what is required.

You must, at all times, observe all relevant health and safety precautions.

Time allowed: 2 hours

Introduction

This assignment is broken down into 2 parts:

1 Task A requires candidates to create a spreadsheet from a user description and enter appropriate formulas.

2 Task B requires candidates to edit the spreadsheet produced for Task A.

Scenario

You work for a magazine that runs occasional articles on home finance, loans and savings. This month you are helping to research an article on savings accounts.

You are asked to create a spreadsheet to display the net annual interest rates for several savings accounts. Some of the accounts give a higher interest rate to people who invest larger amounts of money, so you should show interest rates for investment amounts of £100, £500 and £1000. The spreadsheet should calculate the amount of interest to be added at the end of the year for each account and for each investment amount. There will also be a section showing how the best buy compares with the worst buy for each investment amount.

Use the sample in the figure as a guide to the design of your spreadsheet. Choose suitable fonts and sizes. Use bold for emphasis. Try to line up column headings over their contents. Titles might be centred.

Savings Accounts							
		Amount	100	Amount	500	Amount	1000
Bank/Building Society	Account name	Rate	Added	Rate	Added	Rate	Added
Allied Investments	bonus 60	1.25%		1.50%		1.75%	
Counties Bank	postal direct	2.50%		2.50%		2.50%	
Cragside BS	e-saver	2.25%		2.50%		3%	
Southampton BS	direct 30	2%		2.75%		3.20%	
Worldwide BS	bonus saver	2%		2.60%		3.30%	
Best buy							
Worst buy							
Difference							

Figure 6.2 Sample savings account spreadsheet

Task A

1 Start up the spreadsheet software and start a new spreadsheet.
2 Create the spreadsheet. Base it on Figure 6.2 and take account of the guidance notes in the scenario.
3 Format the cells which will contain money to currency with 2 decimal places.
4 Enter a formula to calculate the amount of interest to be added to £100 in the Allied Investments account. Use an absolute reference (with $ signs) to the cell containing £100.
5 Copy the formula down the column to calculate the interest to be added to £100 in the other accounts.
6 Enter formulas to calculate the interest added to £500 and to £1000. Replicate (copy) these formulas down their columns.
7 Either put borders round your cells or set the gridlines to show in printouts.
8 Key in your name in a spare cell and save your spreadsheet as Savings Accounts.xls.
9 Print the spreadsheet on one sheet of paper and write 'Printout 1' on it.

Task B

1 Southampton BS has withdrawn their direct 30 account, so delete the whole row. Do not leave the row with empty cells.
2 Insert a new row between Allied Investments and Counties Bank. Enter new data. Barnwood Bank has an account called e-savings. The interest rates are 2.3% for £100, 2.7% for £500 and 3.1% for £1000.
3 Replicate formulas to find the interest added to each amount in the new account.
4 In the Best Buy row, and in the column showing amounts of interest for £100, enter a formula to calculate the maximum amount of interest added for £100.
5 In the Best Buy row, enter formulas to find the maximum amount of interest added for £500 and for £1000.
6 In the Worst Buy row, enter formulas to find the minimum amount of interest added for £100, for £500 and for £1000.
7 In the Difference row, enter formulas to subtract the minimum amount from the maximum amount of interest for £100, for £500 and for £1000.
8 Save your spreadsheet as Savings Accounts2.xls.
9 Print your spreadsheet using one sheet of paper. Write 'Printout 2' on the paper.
10 Print your spreadsheet showing the formulas. Write 'Printout 3' on the paper.
11 Save a copy of both your spreadsheets on to a floppy disk.
12 Close down the spreadsheet software.

Note:
- At the conclusion of this assignment, hand all paperwork and disks to the test supervisor.
- Ensure that your name is on the disk (if using a floppy disk) and all documentation.
- If the assignment is taken over more than one period, all floppy disks and paperwork must be returned to the test supervisor at the end of each sitting.

Solutions

This section gives sample answers to all the 'Check your knowledge' questions. It also gives the final versions of spreadsheets from the skills practice, consolidation exercises and practice assignments. Formulas are provided where necessary. Your own solutions may differ a little from the sample solutions but still be correct.

Section 1 Spreadsheets, software and hardware

Check your knowledge

1 You can change the numbers and the computer will calculate the new results.
2 Microsoft Excel, Lotus 1-2-3. You may have chosen others.
3 A keyboard and a pointing device such as a mouse.
4 You will need to measure the monitor for yourself. Measure diagonally, corner to corner. The screen size may be anything from 15 inches to 21 inches.
5 You will need to go and look at the printer and maybe ask. You are most likely to be using a laser printer or an inkjet printer.
6 Computer output on paper.
7 The answer may be obvious. If not, then ask your tutor. If your computer is linked by cables to other computers and you have to log on at the start of the session then you are working on a networked computer.
8 A workbook.
9 Standard toolbar and Formatting toolbar.
10 Take regular breaks away from the screen. (You may also know other precautions.)

Section 2 Creating a new spreadsheet

Practise your skills 1 – Stalls spreadsheet

	A	B
1	Stalls	
2		
3	Income	
4	Cakes	89.25
5	Plants	62.32
6	Raffle	96.75
7	Tombola	84.35
8	Total	332.67
9		
10	Expenses	
11	Band	57.75
12	Prizes	43.15
13	Tickets	6.35
14	Total	107.25
15		
16	Profit	225.42
17		

Figure 7.1 Stalls spreadsheet solution

You should also have a formulas printout including the following formulas:

Cell B8 =SUM(B4:B7)
Cell B14 =SUM(B11:B13)
Cell B16 =B8-B14

Practise your skills 2 – Computer sales spreadsheet

	A	B	C	D	E	F
1	Sales					
2						
3					Nasir	Sarah
4			Model	System X	25300	21150
5				HomePro	18750	22800
6				Total	44050	43950
7						
8	Bonus	2%		Bonus	881	879
9						

Figure 7.2 Computer Sales spreadsheet solution

You should also have a formulas printout including the following formulas:

Cell E6 =SUM(E4:E5)
Cell F6 =SUM(F4:F5)
Cell E8 =E6*B8
Cell F8 =F6*B8

Check your knowledge

1 Text (or labels), Numbers (or values) and Formulas
2 **a** and **c**
3 =
4 =C5*C6
5 =SUM(D3:D8)
6 /
7 –
8 .xls
9 The computer's memory is volatile. It loses its contents when the power supply is turned off. You save your work to disk to put it in long-term storage.
10 landscape

Section 3 Altering an existing spreadsheet

Practise your skills 1 – Clothes spreadsheet

	A	B	C	D	E
1	*Clothes*				
2					
3		VAT rate	17.50%		
4					
5	Code	Item	Price	Quantity	Cost
6	M32	T shirt	£ 6.99	6	£ 41.94
7	M26	Jeans	£ 17.99	3	£ 53.97
8				Subtotal	£ 95.91
9				VAT	£ 16.78
10				Total	£ 112.69
11					

Figure 7.3 Clothes2 spreadsheet solution

Practise your skills 2 – Stalls spreadsheet

	A	B	C
1	**Summer Fete 2002**		
2			
3	**Income**		
4	Cakes	£ 89.25	
5	Plants	£ 62.32	
6	Raffle	£ 97.65	
7	Tombola	£ 84.35	
8	**Total**	**£ 333.57**	
9			
10	**Expenses**		
11	Band	£ 57.75	
12	Prizes	£ 43.15	
13	Tickets	£ 6.35	
14	**Total**	**£ 107.25**	
15			
16	**Profit**	**£ 226.32**	
17			

Figure 7.4 Stalls2 spreadsheet solution

Check your knowledge

1 To save and replace the old spreadsheet you click the Save button on the toolbar.
2 To save the new version of the spreadsheet as a separate file, you click on the File menu and choose Save As from the drop down list. You then give your spreadsheet a new name and click Save.
3 Budget2002
4 Editing
5 Formatting
6 A cell that contains a formula normally displays the result of the formula, not the formula itself. Formatting can also make the appearance different to the content. For example, a cell containing the number 0.2 can be formatted to display 20% or £ 0.20.

Consolidation 1 DIY invoice

Ryedale DIY Store

Item code	Item name	Unit price	Number	Cost
H12	2 L Gloss Paint	£ 3.20	2	£ 6.40
T24	5 L Emulsion Paint	£ 5.50	3	£ 16.50
P96	Roller	£ 4.00	1	£ 4.00
P33	Brush size 2	£ 2.50	2	£ 5.00
P36	Brush size 5	£ 3.15	2	£ 6.30
			Subtotal	£ 38.20
			Discount	£ 1.91
			Total	£ 36.29

5% Discount

Figure 7.5 DIY Invoice spreadsheet solution

Section 4 Copying, inserting rows and choosing what to print

Practise your skills 1 – Clothes spreadsheet

Clothes

		VAT rate			17.50%			

Code	Item		Price	Quantity		Cost
M32	T shirt	£	6.99	6	£	41.94
M21	Socks	£	1.50	5	£	7.50
M35	Sweatshirt	£	14.99	1	£	14.99
M26	Jeans	£	17.99	3	£	53.97
				Subtotal	£	118.40
				VAT	£	20.72
				Total	**£**	**139.12**

Figure 7.6 Clothes3 spreadsheet solution

Practise your skills 2 – Stalls spreadsheet

Summer Fete 2002

Income		
Cakes	£	89.25
Raffle	£	97.65
Plants	£	62.32
Book	£	24.20
Tombola	£	84.35
Total	**£**	**357.77**

Expenses		
Band	£	57.75
Tickets	£	6.35
Total	**£**	**64.10**

Profit	£	293.67

Figure 7.7 Stalls3 spreadsheet solution

Check your knowledge

1 above
2 6
3 nothing
4 On the row number at the left of the row
5 A pop-up menu of commands
6 =SUM(H2:H4)
7 =C14*D14
8 =$C$12*D14
9 They will get even narrower when you change back to the Normal view with results, and you will need to adjust them.
10 Selection

Consolidation 2 Expense claim. Final version of spreadsheet

Expense claim form

By car

	Date	Destination		Miles	Mileage rate			Claim
	21/03/02	Gloucester		82	£	0.50	£	41.00
	03/04/02	Gloucester		82	£	0.50	£	41.00
	28/03/02	Gloucester		82	£	0.50	£	41.00
	22/03/02	Gloucester		82	£	0.50	£	41.00

Public transport

	Date	Destination		Train/bus etc		Fare
	26/03/02	London		Train	£	36.50

				Total	£	200.50

Figure 7.8 Final version of Expense claim spreadsheet

	E
5	=C5*D5
6	=C6*D6
7	=C7*D7
8	=C8*D8
9	
10	
11	Fare
12	36.5
13	
14	=SUM(E5:E13)

Figure 7.9 Formulas from Expense claim spreadsheet

Section 5 Producing a spreadsheet from your own design

Practise your skills 1

Your design might look like Figure 7.10 and your spreadsheet might look like Figure 7.11, but there are many other possibilities for formatting. You should also have a printout showing formulas.

	A	B	C	D
1	Police Authority Spending			
2				
3		2000/01	2001/02	2002/03
4		£ thousands	£ thousands	£ thousands
5	Police pay	100377	120109	120338
6	Pensions	18390	19804	21765
7	Civilian staff	32670	41566	50927
8	Training	1993	2018	2061
9	Other	48328	49918	58201
10	Total	=SUM(B5:B9)	copy	→

Main text Arial 10
Heading Arial MT Black 12

A5 to A10 bold left align
B3 to D3 bold right align
B4 to D4 right align

B5 to D10 number, no decimal places

Widths A: 17, B-D: 12.5

Figure 7.10 Design of Police Spending spreadsheet

Police Authority Spending

	2000/01 £ thousands	2001/02 £ thousands	2002/03 £ thousands
Police pay	100377	120109	120338
Pensions	18390	19804	21765
Civilian staff	32670	41566	50927
Training	1993	2018	2061
Other	48328	49918	58201
Total	201758	233415	253292

Figure 7.11 Police Spending spreadsheet solution

Practise your skills 2

Your spreadsheet might look like Figure 7.12. You may have chosen alternative fonts and formatting. You should also have a handwritten design and a printout showing formulas.

Sharing a meal

Chicken in black bean sauce	£	5.20
Sweet and sour pork	£	5.25
Beef with mushroom	£	5.75
Stir fried vegetables	£	5.00
Fried rice for four	£	6.00
Total	£	27.20

Share	£	6.80

Figure 7.12 Sharing a Meal spreadsheet solution

Practise your skills 3

Your spreadsheet might look like Figure 7.13. You may have chosen alternative fonts and formatting. You should also have a handwritten design and a printout of formulas.

Temperatures

Time	Sun	Mon	Tues	Weds	Thurs	Fri	Sat
02:00	5	4	-1	0	3	5	2
08:00	9	8	8	10	12	15	10
14:00	20	22	18	16	20	28	22
20:00	14	15	12	11	15	17	15

Maximum	20	22	18	16	20	28	22
Minimum	5	4	-1	0	3	5	2
Average	12	12.25	9.25	9.25	12.5	16.25	12.25

Weekly summary

Maximum	28
Minimum	-1
Average	11.96

Figure 7.13 Temperatures spreadsheet solution

Formulas should be something like this, but the cell references may differ, depending on which cells you have used for entering data.

=MAX(B4:B7)

=MIN(B4:B7)

=AVERAGE(B4:B7)

Practise your skills 4

Your answer might look like Figure 7.14. You may have chosen alternative fonts and formatting. You should also have a handwritten design and a printout of formulas.

Selling costs of printed items			
Item	Cost price	Markup	Selling price
T shirt	£ 3.00	5%	£ 3.15
Sweatshirt	£ 11.00	2%	£ 11.22
Cap	£ 6.00	10%	£ 6.60
Bag	£ 8.00	4%	£ 8.32

Figure 7.14 Selling Costs spreadsheet solution

The formula for the selling price of a T-shirt is =B4+B4*C4. You will have different cell references if you have put the T-shirt figures in a different row.

Check your knowledge

1 5
2 40
3 54
4 70
5 19
6 People are more likely to make mistakes in complicated formulas.

Practice assignments

Practice assignment 1

You should have a handwritten design and four printouts.

SavePlus

Part time employees' wages
Week starting: 30/09/02

Name	Hours worked Mon-Fri	Sat	Sun	Total hours	Hourly rate	Pay for week
Evans E	22	0	0	22	£ 4.25	£ 93.50
Jones H	17	6	6	29	£ 5.30	£ 153.70
Jones T	8	4	4	16	£ 5.30	£ 84.80
Owen G	10	5	4	19	£ 5.75	£ 109.25
Price C	25	0	0	25	£ 5.75	£ 143.75
Rees J	30	0	0	30	£ 6.20	£ 186.00
Thomas S	10	6	5	21	£ 5.75	£ 120.75
					Total:	£ 891.75

Printout 1

Figure 7.15 SavePlus printout 1

Part time employees' wages
Week starting: 30/09/02 (today's date)

Name	Hours worked Mon-Fri	Sat	Sun	Total hours	Hourly rate		Pay for week	
Ward S (own name)	22	0	0	22	£	6.20	£	136.40
Jones H	17	6	6	29	£	5.30	£	153.70
Jones T	8	4	4	16	£	5.30	£	84.80
Owen G	10	5	4	19	£	5.75	£	109.25
Price C	25	0	0	25	£	5.75	£	143.75
Rees J	30	0	0	30	£	6.20	£	186.00
Thomas S	10	6	5	21	£	5.75	£	120.75
					Total:		£	934.65

Printout 2

Figure 7.16 SavePlus printout 2

Part time employees' wages
Week starting: 30/09/02 (today's date)

Name	Hours worked Mon-Fri	Sat	Sun	Total hours	Hourly rate		Pay for week	
Jones H	17	6	6	29	£	5.30	£	153.70
Ward S (own name)	22	0	0	22	£	6.20	£	136.40
Jones T	8	4	4	16	£	5.30	£	84.80
Owen G	10	5	4	19	£	5.75	£	109.25
Price C	25	0	0	25	£	5.75	£	143.75
Rees J	30	0	0	30	£	6.20	£	186.00
Thomas S	10	6	5	21	£	5.75	£	120.75
					Total:		£	934.65

Printout 3

Figure 7.17 SavePlus printout 3

	E	F	G
6	Total	Hourly	Pay for
7	hours	rate	week
8	=SUM(B8:D8)	5.3	=E8*F8
9	=SUM(B9:D9)	6.2	=E9*F9
10	=SUM(B10:D10)	5.3	=E10*F10
11	=SUM(B11:D11)	5.75	=E11*F11
12	=SUM(B12:D12)	5.75	=E12*F12
13	=SUM(B13:D13)	6.2	=E13*F13
14	=SUM(B14:D14)	5.75	=E14*F14
15		Total:	=SUM(G8:G14)
16	Printout 4		

Figure 7.18 SavePlus printout 4

Practice assignment 2

There should be a handwritten design and four printouts.

Pay and bonus					BONUS1	
Name		Sales	Bonus rate	Basic pay	Pay with bonus	
N James	£	43,200	0.20%	£ 1,200.00	£ 1,286.40	
D Lee	£	58,360	0.50%	£ 1,200.00	£ 1,491.80	
W Matthews	£	20,906	0.50%	£ 1,350.00	£ 1,454.53	
G Rogers	£	62,400	0.20%	£ 1,350.00	£ 1,474.80	
M Yau	£	53,180	0.20%	£ 1,400.00	£ 1,506.36	
				Total	£ 7,213.89	

Figure 7.19 Bonus printout 1

Pay and bonus				BONUS1 formulas
Name	Sales	Bonus rate	Basic pay	Pay with bonus
N James	43200	0.002	1200	=B4*C4+D4
D Lee	58360	0.005	1200	=B5*C5+D5
W Matthews	20906	0.005	1350	=B6*C6+D6
G Rogers	62400	0.002	1350	=B7*C7+D7
M Yau	53180	0.002	1400	=B8*C8+D8
			Total	=SUM(E4:E8)

Figure 7.20 Bonus printout 2

						BONUS2	
Name		Sales	Bonus rate	Basic pay	Pay with bonus	Deductions	
N James	£	38,750	0.20%	£ 1,200.00	£ 1,277.50	£ 255.50
D Lee	£	51,600	0.50%	£ 1,200.00	£ 1,458.00	£ 291.60
W Matthews	£	29,603	0.50%	£ 1,350.00	£ 1,498.02	£ 299.60
P Nolan	£	31,947	0.20%	£ 1,400.00	£ 1,463.89	£ 292.78
G Rogers	£	55,400	0.20%	£ 1,350.00	£ 1,460.80	£ 292.16
M Yau	£	48,000	0.20%	£ 1,400.00	£ 1,496.00	£ 299.20
				Total	£ 8,654.21	£ 1,730.84

Figure 7.21 Bonus printout 3

Pay and bonus					BONUS3	
Name		Sales	Bonus rate	Basic pay	Pay with bonus	
N James	£	43,200	0.20%	£ 1,200.00	£ 1,286.40	
D Lee	£	58,360	0.50%	£ 1,200.00	£ 1,491.80	
W Matthews	£	20,906	0.50%	£ 1,350.00	£ 1,454.53	
G Rogers	£	62,400	0.20%	£ 1,350.00	£ 1,474.80	
M Yau	£	53,180	0.20%	£ 1,400.00	£ 1,506.36	
				Total	£ 7,213.89	
Name		Sales	Bonus rate	Basic pay	Pay with bonus	Deductions
N James	£	38,750	0.20%	£ 1,200.00	£ 1,277.50	£ 255.50
W Matthews	£	29,603	0.50%	£ 1,350.00	£ 1,498.02	£ 299.60
P Nolan	£	31,947	0.20%	£ 1,400.00	£ 1,463.89	£ 292.78
G Rogers	£	55,400	0.20%	£ 1,350.00	£ 1,460.80	£ 292.16
M Yau	£	48,000	0.20%	£ 1,400.00	£ 1,496.00	£ 299.20
				Total	£ 7,196.21	£ 1,439.24

Figure 7.22 Bonus printout 4

Practice assignment 3

You should have three printouts.

Savings Accounts							
		Amount	£ 100.00	Amount	£ 500.00	Amount	£ 1,000.00
Bank/Building Society	Account name	Rate	Added	Rate	Added	Rate	Added
Allied Investments	bonus 60	1.25%	£ 1.25	1.50%	£ 7.50	1.75%	£ 17.50
Counties Bank	postal direct	2.50%	£ 2.50	2.50%	£ 12.50	2.50%	£ 25.00
Cragside BS	e-saver	2.25%	£ 2.25	2.50%	£ 12.50	3%	£ 30.00
Southampton BS	direct 30	2%	£ 2.00	2.75%	£ 13.75	3.20%	£ 32.00
Worldwide BS	bonus saver	2%	£ 2.00	2.60%	£ 13.00	3.30%	£ 33.00
Best buy							
Worst buy							
Difference							

Figure 7.23 Savings accounts printout 1

Savings Accounts							
		Amount	£100.00	Amount	£500.00	Amount	£1,000.00
Bank/Building Society	Account name	Rate	Added	Rate	Added	Rate	Added
Allied Investments	bonus 60	1.25%	£ 1.25	1.50%	£ 7.50	1.75%	£ 17.50
Barnwood Bank	e-savings	2.30%	£ 2.30	2.70%	£ 13.50	3.10%	£ 31.00
Counties Bank	postal direct	2.50%	£ 2.50	2.50%	£ 12.50	2.50%	£ 25.00
Cragside BS	e-saver	2.25%	£ 2.25	2.50%	£ 12.50	3%	£ 30.00
Worldwide BS	bonus saver	2%	£ 2.00	2.60%	£ 13.00	3.30%	£ 33.00
Best buy			£ 2.50		£ 13.50		£ 33.00
Worst buy			£ 1.25		£ 7.50		£ 17.50
Difference			£ 1.25		£ 6.00		£ 15.50

Figure 7.24 Savings accounts printout 2

Savings Accou							
		Amount		100	Amount	500	Amount	1000
Bank/Building Society	Account name	Rate	Added	Rate	Added	Rate	Added
Allied Investments	bonus 60	0.0125	=C5*$D$3	0.015	=E5*$F$3	0.0175	=G5*$H$3
Barnwood Bank	e-savings	0.023	=C6*$D$3	0.027	=E6*$F$3	0.031	=G6*$H$3
Counties Bank	postal direct	0.025	=C7*$D$3	0.025	=E7*$F$3	0.025	=G7*$H$3
Cragside BS	e-saver	0.0225	=C8*$D$3	0.025	=E8*$F$3	0.03	=G8*$H$3
Worldwide BS	bonus saver	0.02	=C9*$D$3	0.026	=E9*$F$3	0.033	=G9*$H$3
Best buy			=MAX(D5:D9)		=MAX(F5:F9)		=MAX(H5:H9)
Worst buy			=MIN(D5:D9)		=MIN(F5:F9)		=MIN(H5:H9)
Difference			=D11-D12		=F11-F12		=H11-H12

Figure 7.25 Savings accounts printout 3

Outcomes matching guide

All the City & Guilds outcomes for Spreadsheets are covered.

1.1	load spreadsheet software	Section 1 Task 1.2
1.2	open previously prepared spreadsheets	Section 3 Task 3.1
1.3	navigate around spreadsheets using the keyboard and/or a pointing device	Section 1 Task 1.5
1.4	select cells in spreadsheets using the keyboard and/or a pointing device	Section 3 Task 3.8
1.5	save spreadsheets in the correct format	Section 2 Task 2.7
1.6	print on an appropriate output device	Section 2 Task 2.8
1.7	close the spreadsheet software	Section 1 Task 1.10
K1.1	identify the hardware requirements for efficient use of a spreadsheet software package	Section 1 Information: hardware for spreadsheets
K1.2	identify typical filenames and extensions for spreadsheets	Section 2 Information: filenames
K1.3	identify appropriate printing facilities for providing different forms of hard copy of a spreadsheet	Section 1 Information: hardware for spreadsheets
2.1	plan a spreadsheet layout for a given specification	Section 5 Tasks 5.1, 5.2
2.2	choose suitable layouts and formats for data	Section 5 Task 5.3
2.3	choose suitable titles and labels	Section 5 Task 5.2
2.4	construct suitable formulas for calculated cells	Section 5 Task 5.4
2.5	identify the printout required for a given spreadsheet	Section 5 Task 5.5
K2.1	identify text/label and numeric data	Section 2 Information: text and numbers
K2.2	identify the difference between the contents of a cell and its appearance: formulas/outcomes, justification of numeric/text	Section 2 Information: cell contents and appearance
K2.3	identify the need for clear titles: data rows, columns	Section 5 Information: the design
K2.4	describe how formulas are constructed	Section 5 Information: formulas
3.1	create spreadsheets according to a given design • insert text into spreadsheet cells • insert numbers into spreadsheet cells • insert simple formulas and functions into spreadsheet cells using: buttons, menus, pointing device and keyboard	Section 2 Tasks 2.1, 2.2, 2.3, 2.4, 2.16, 2.17, 2.24 Section 4 Task 4.10 Section 5 Task 5.13
3.2	align cell contents: right, left and centre	Section 3 Task 3.9
3.3	modify cell width and height	Section 3 Task 3.7
3.4	modify number formats: general, fixed decimal places, percentage	Section 3 Task 3.10
3.5	modify text attributes: font, size, enhancement	Section 3 Task 3.11

4.1	insert rows and columns into spreadsheet	Section 4 Tasks 4.2, 4.6
4.2	delete rows and columns from spreadsheet	Section 4 Tasks 4.5, 4.7
4.3	move and copy ranges of cells	Section 4 Tasks 4.3, 4.4
4.4	delete cell contents	Section 3 Task 3.6
4.5	replicate formulas	Section 4 Task 4.10
4.6	edit the contents of individual cells	Section 3 Tasks 3.4, 3.5
4.7	use the undo feature	Section 3 Task 3.12
5.1	use saving processes to prevent loss of work: frequent, automatic	Section 3 Task 3.3
5.2	use systematic filenames and extensions to save edited spreadsheets	Section 3 Task 3.2
5.3	produce hard copy of a spreadsheet, and of selected areas of a spreadsheet on single sheets of paper according to a given design	Section 4 Tasks 4.14, 4.15
5.4	produce hard copy showing formulas	Section 2 Task 2.9
K5.1	describe the problems provided by software where all the data is held in volatile memory	Section 2 Information: saving to disk
K5.2	identify the importance of using suitable filenames for developing versions of spreadsheets	Section 3 Information: spreadsheet versions

Quick reference guide

Most tasks can be carried out in more than one way.
- Select a command from a drop down menu
- Click a toolbar button
- Use a hotkey or keyboard shortcut
- Right click and select a command from a pop-up menu.

Here are some alternative methods for carrying out common tasks.

Task	Toolbar button	Menu command	Hotkey
Create a new spreadsheet		File menu New ...	Ctrl + n
Open an existing spreadsheet		File menu Open ...	Ctrl + o
Save a spreadsheet		File menu Save ...	Ctrl + s
Save another copy of a spreadsheet with a new name		File menu Save As ...	Shift + F12
Preview a spreadsheet		File menu Print Preview	
Print a spreadsheet		File menu Print ...	Ctrl + p
Set up page for printing: gridlines, headings, fit to size, orientation, header/footer		File menu Page Setup	
Show formulas		Tools menu, Options, View, Formulas	
Cut selected cell contents to clipboard		Edit menu Cut	Ctrl + x
Copy selected cell contents to clipboard		Edit menu Copy	Ctrl + c
Paste from clipboard to selected cell		Edit menu Paste	Ctrl + v
Delete selected cell contents		Edit menu Clear ...	Delete
Undo last action		Edit menu Undo	Ctrl + z
Make contents of selected cell(s) bold	**B**	Format menu Cells, Font ...	Ctrl + b
Make contents of selected cell(s) italic	*I*	Format menu Cells, Font ...	Ctrl + i
Change font of selected cell	Arial	Format menu Cells, Font ...	Ctrl + 1
Change font size of selected cell	10	Format menu Cells, Font ...	Ctrl + 1

Align left in selected cell(s)			Format menu Cells, Alignment . . .	Ctrl + 1
Align right in selected cell(s)			Format menu Cells, Alignment . . .	Ctrl + 1
Align centre in selected cell(s)			Format menu Cells, Alignment . . .	Ctrl + 1
Format selected cell to currency			Format menu Cells, Number . . .	Ctrl + 1
Increase decimal places in selected cell			Format menu Cells, Number . . .	
Decrease decimal places in selected cell			Format menu Cells, Number . . .	
Change column width	Point to border between column headings and drag or double click		Format menu Column, Width . . .	
Insert row above selected row			Insert menu Rows	
Delete selected row			Edit menu Delete	
Add values in column/row with Autosum				

Calculations:

=	starts formula		
+	add	e.g. =B3+B4	
−	subtract	e.g. =B3−B4	
*	multiply	e.g. =B3*B4	
/	divide	e.g. =B3/B4	
SUM()	adds contents of range of cells in brackets	e.g. =SUM(B3:B7)	
AVERAGE()	finds average of contents of range of cells in brackets	e.g. =AVERAGE(B3:B7)	
MAX()	finds largest value in range of cells in brackets	e.g. =MAX(B3:B7)	
MIN()	finds smallest value in range of cells in brackets	e.g. =MIN(B3:B7)	